# UNDERSTANDING AND ADJUSTING SEWING PATTERNS

*to make clothes that fit and flatter*

# UNDERSTANDING AND ADJUSTING SEWING PATTERNS
## *to make clothes that fit and flatter*

### GILL MCBRIDE

THE CROWOOD PRESS

First published in 2018 by
The Crowood Press Ltd
Ramsbury, Marlborough
Wiltshire SN8 2HR

**www.crowood.com**

**British Library Cataloguing-in-Publication Data**
A catalogue record for this book is available from the British Library.

ISBN 978 1 78500 447 6

**Acknowledgements**
I would like to thank the following sewing students for their help with the photographs: Christine, Rita, Ros, Nicola and Mandy. Thanks to Jane Hunter of Hunters Atelier, for help with the photographs and diagrams.

Typeset by Jean Cussons Typesetting, Diss, Norfolk
Printed and bound in India by Replika Press Pvt Ltd

# CONTENTS

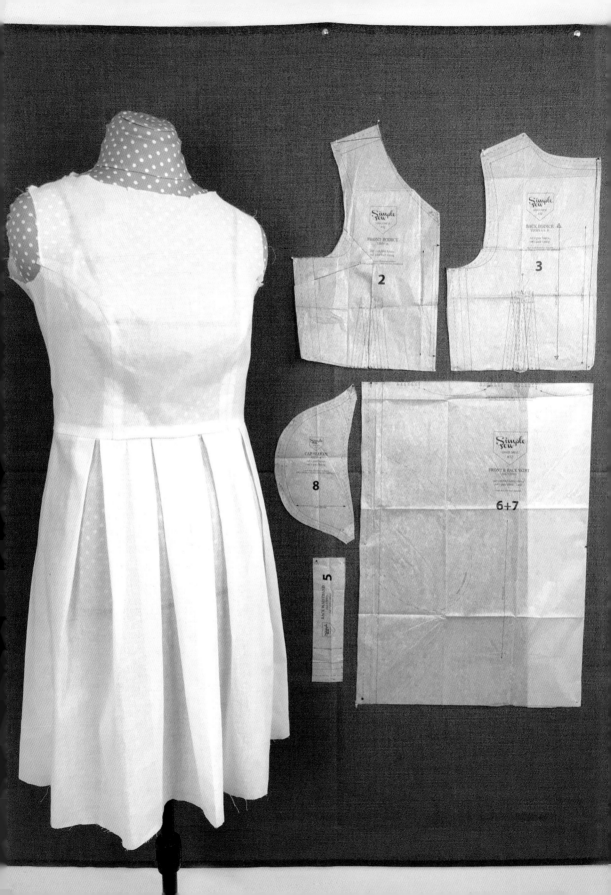

# INTRODUCTION

When a well-dressed person passes by, you will always notice them. They look good, walk tall and clearly feel good about themselves.

The clothes we wear reflect the mood we are in. How often have you stood in front of the wardrobe, doors open, looking at the clothes hanging inside and you can't decide what to wear. You can't find the right garment to suit your mood for the day. On the other hand, you may need to dress to suit the things you will be doing that day. If you are going to have a lazy day at home, you'll probably choose comfortable casuals, such as soft trousers, a sloppy sweater or a loose T-shirt. If you are going to an important meeting, a smart skirt and blouse with a nice fitted jacket might be your choice. Whatever the day holds, your clothes are an important reflection of who you are and who you want to be. Knowing that your clothes fit well and that you look good in them can boost your mood, no matter what you are doing.

It's so infuriating when we see something in a shop that we love, but it just doesn't fit us properly. We might try the garment on, only to find that the darts are in the wrong place, the waistline is too high, the bust is too tight or too big, the length is wrong or the waist/hips don't fit. Sometimes we can buy a new garment and take it home and fix it so that it does fit us better, but how annoying is it that we have to alter a ready-to-wear garment.

Fitting is key. Clothes that fit well make us feel good, make us look good and give us confidence. When we wear a garment that doesn't fit just right, we end up tugging at the hem, pulling at the waist, fixing the shoulders and so on. Sometimes we are not aware of this constant rearranging of our clothes. But if we examine our wardrobe and pick out the garments that we feel really good wearing, this is probably because they fit well and we feel very comfortable in them.

It is the same when making your own clothes. Fitting is key. We buy a pattern, we cut it out and we make a new dress/jacket/trousers. Then we try the garment on and it may be OK, but not quite right. Luckily, we have made the garment in calico first! So we haven't ruined our gorgeous fabric on a garment that doesn't fit properly. We take our calico toile (also called a muslin, and sometimes a fitting garment or test garment) and we begin to make fitting adjustments. Once we have achieved what we want in terms of fit and design, we then transfer all those adjustments to the paper pattern, ready to cut out the garment proper in our gorgeous fabric. That's how fitting works.

Shape and size don't matter. Fitting is necessary for big and little, cuddly and slim, tall and short people. Once the fit is right, though, the garment will look great. A well-dressed person wearing well-fitting clothes is just that. We don't notice size or shape when we are looking at someone who is wearing beautifully fitted clothes. Well-fitted clothes enhance everybody.

## Is Fitting Difficult?

There is a lot of anxiety around fitting. Many of us think we can't do it. There are lots of books on fitting and many of them make it seem very technical and very specialized, and this is also sometimes the case if the garment being fitted has a demanding design and unusual construction methods. But actually, anyone can learn how to fit the kind of clothes that we make at home for ourselves and our families. All it takes is time, a bit of judgement, common sense and growing confidence. The more you do it, the more you will learn about fitting and the more confident you will become about actually doing it. If we learn about the most common fitting issues concerning bust, hips, shoulders and trousers, that will allow us to fit almost all garments on ourselves and others to a really good standard. Once we are confident with those fitting issues, then our ability to recognize finer fitting issues will increase, and our fitting solutions will improve and also become more creative.

## Learn Your Own Methods of Fitting

All commercial patterns come with lengthen/shorten lines. It is sensible to use them if the length of the garment you are fitting is not right, because they have been placed on the garment in an area that will not affect the style. For instance, there are often lengthen/shorten lines below the bust, below the hips, above the knee and above and below the elbow on sleeves. Use these lines if they are in the right place and they produce the desired result.

However, if you are fitting a garment on someone who is long from waist to hip, then you will almost certainly need to lengthen the dress, skirt or trousers between the waist and hip. The same applies to someone who is long from shoulder to bust apex/bust point. If the garment needs to be lengthened or shortened at either of those places – or any other part of the garment – then make the adjustment on the pattern at the point where you think it is going to produce the best result. Don't always rely solely on the guidelines given on the pattern pieces if you think there is a better alternative.

There is no right or wrong way of fitting. There are lots of guidelines and there are many traditional and accepted ways of fitting. There are also many sensible and straightforward ways of fitting. For instance, many people will feel apprehensive about making a full bust adjustment. It seems very complicated and many of us will try and avoid doing one. But actually, the traditional method of making a full bust adjustment can work very well on garments with both darts and princess seams. Once you understand the principle and have completed your first adjustment, the fear of making this adjustment is removed. You will tackle your next one much more confidently, and the door will be opened to you for making many more garments with darts and princess seams.

There are also less traditional, more creative ways of making fitting adjustments that work well for lots of fitting issues, and there is a lot of information available describing those more creative methods and the philosophy behind them. The key thing is that you understand the principle behind the method you have chosen and you can follow the method. Decide which way suits you best for each individual fitting issue and use it. Ultimately, if you do enough fittings, you will find your own preferred methods, and your growing confidence will allow you to make judgements about how to fit each individual garment on different people. You will probably end up using a mix of traditional methods and some that you have developed yourself because they work for you and get good results.

This applies equally to those of us who prefer to sew only for ourselves and our family, and to those who use a dressform to fit garments. We look at books and use methods that we think we can follow and that we think will work for us, and eventually we also end up using methods that we have developed ourselves.

# The Tools for Fitting

You will start with your chosen pattern and a length of calico. It is best to use a medium to lightweight calico as it drapes and fits the body reasonably well. It is also good for marking with a marker pen and it presses quite well. A heavy calico will be quite stiff and not so easy to work with. However, if you are making something that will be sewn in a stretch fabric, then calico won't work. You will need to buy some stretch fabric that will be similar in characteristics to your final chosen fabric to make your toile.

Once you have made your toile and have completed some of the fitting exercises, then you will need particular tools. These include:

**French curve.** This is a drafting ruler that is shaped a bit like a giant apostrophe! The curves on it are graded and there is also a straight-line ruler on one side. French curves come with either metric measurements (centimetres) or imperial measurements (inches), so make sure you buy the right one for you. This tool is used for marking new curves and lines on paper patterns and is invaluable. Many people draw freehand curves, but the French curve allows you to do a far better job.

**Tape measure.** Always an essential tool in the sewing room.

**Pattern tissue.** This can be purchased tissue or it can be all those large pieces that you would normally throw away when cutting out your pattern. Keep them in a handy box because they are extremely useful for making pattern alterations.

**Sticky tape.** Look for a 'magic' tape that you can write on. This is the best type to use on pattern tissue and can also be used on your fabrics – for instance, to mark the wrong side when both right and wrong sides look identical. It doesn't mark your fabric when you remove it.

**Marker pen.** These are important for mark-ing alterations on your toile. Even though alter-

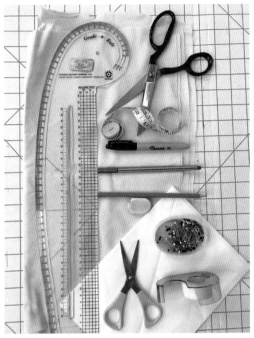

**Fig. 1   Tools needed for fitting.**

ations and adjustments are pinned in, they are usually also marked on the toile with marker pen. Any colour is good!

**Fine-tipped pen.** Invaluable for marking permanent alterations on the pattern tissue.

**Pencil and eraser.** Draw in new curves and lines with a pencil before going over them with the fine-tipped pen.

**Paper scissors.** An essential – in order to protect those precious fabric scissors!

Fitting is a learning process. The more you do it, the more comfortable you will be with making personal fitting adjustments to a garment either for yourself or for someone else. Your fitting skills will improve the more you use them, and you will become more creative with your fitting skills and understand that there is no one particular way to solve a fitting problem. It's important to work with the fabric and the person who is being fitted, and it's important to know how the wearer wants the final garment to look. Be confident and enjoy fitting!

# THE PATTERN

When we buy a pattern, we have usually done so because we love the picture on the front. The style, the fabric, the drape, the shape – whatever it is has said to us: 'make me!' But how do we know if that pattern is actually what we want, that it will suit us, or even if we can actually make it?

We can find out if the pattern will work for us by using the information given on the pattern envelope. There are two elements to the pattern envelope – the front cover and the back cover – and there is a lot of information on both. We need to read this information carefully before we buy the pattern, and especially before we invest in some gorgeous fabric to make the garment.

**Fig. 2  Pattern envelopes showing garments in photographs and drawings.**

## The Pattern Envelope

The first thing that attracts us to a particular pattern is what we see on the front cover. There may be a lovely photograph of a model in the garment or a really nice drawing. But it also has more important information.

On the envelopes shown in Fig. 2 there is a mixture of photographs and drawings. The photographs give us a much better impression of what the garment will actually look like. Vintage patterns always have drawings of their dresses and coats, and look so wonderful with their tiny waists and voluminous skirts. But it is important to remember that the final garment will look quite different on us than it does in the picture. This can be affected by a number of things.

## Which Pattern House Has Made the Pattern?

The pattern house is the company that has made the pattern, for instance Vogue, Colette, New Look. Is it a well-known pattern house or is it a new one that you've not seen before? It may be a make of pattern that you have used regularly and you know that they fit you without too much adjustment. If it's a new pattern house, then you will have to learn about their sizing and fitting. Many of the new pattern houses have sizing that is a bit different to the more established brands. In addition, the designer of this particular pattern may be different from the in-house designers usually used by the pattern house; this is especially the case with Vogue and McCall patterns. This information will be highlighted on the front of the envelope. Again, it may be a designer that you particularly like or one that you have not seen before, or whose garments you have not made before.

## What Is the Size of the Pattern?

Choosing the right pattern size is vital if you are to avoid lots of fitting problems. When you are buying a new pattern, check carefully on the envelope to see what size pattern you have been given. The size range of the pattern is usually marked at the top of the front of the envelope, as seen in Fig 2 above. Many patterns include all sizes from the smallest to the largest in the same envelope, and some have size ranges such as 6–8–10–12–14 and 16–18–20–22.

It is really important that you are sure what size range is offered on your pattern. It is crucial to remember that the size of garment that we sew is almost always one size, and sometimes two sizes, larger than the size we buy in ready-to-wear. So if your pattern envelope reads sizes 6–14 and you know that you buy a size 12 or 14 in ready-to-wear, then you must check the body measurements on the back of the pattern envelope before you buy it, to ensure it will be big enough. It is much easier to reduce a pattern by one or two sizes than it is to size up.

Many patterns are now also drafted with variable bust fittings. This is great for those who have struggled to make full bust adjustments or small bust adjustments, because the pattern has those different sizes included in the envelope on separate tissue pieces all ready to cut out.

Remember: the size of your pattern is just a number! When you have made your fabulously fitting garment, no one will think about what size it is. They will look at you and admire your wonderful new outfit! So check the size on the front of the envelope before you buy and make sure you buy the right one.

## How Much Does the Pattern Cost?

Finally, the price! Some patterns are very expensive, others not so much. Many of the new designer ranges are at the top end of the price bracket, but if you love that garment and can make it fit you beautifully, then you can use the pattern again and again. So the cost of the pattern becomes less important and you have a wardrobe of clothes that fit and suit you really well.

# The Back of the Envelope

Now we must look at the back of the envelope. For most of us, the back of the envelope is simply about how much fabric we need, and that's sometimes all we look at. However, it gives us more information than this and it's a really good idea to start looking at it more closely. In fact, there is so much information that the pattern house needs to give us that it doesn't always fit on the back of the envelope, so you might find it inside, either on the instruction sheet or on the pattern tissue itself.

## Line Drawings

The first thing we should look at on the back of the pattern envelope is the line drawing of the garment. This is where we can see more clearly which pieces go to make the garment. The line

**Fig. 3   A vintage dress.**

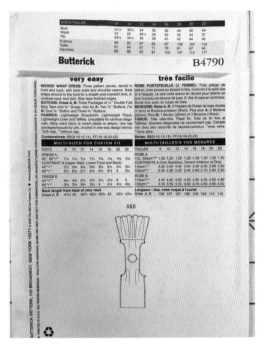

**Fig. 4   How line drawings on the back of the pattern envelope reveal hidden design features.**

drawings may have front and back views, or just back views if the front cover picture is quite clear. Looking at these drawings helps us to understand the construction features and the number of pieces included in the garment. We might then realize that the dress has princess seams that we couldn't discern from the picture on the front, the jacket might have bust darts that we know will never fit us properly, or the trousers might have design and construction features that we're not keen on. Conversely, the line drawings may highlight design features that really appeal to us. They will also show options, such as sleeves, lengths, different neck finishes and a variety of other design features, that are possibly not very clear in the image on the front cover. Examine those line drawings carefully before you decide if the pattern is right for you.

Fig. 4 shows the line drawings for the vintage dress in Fig. 3. How many of us would have realized when we first looked at the drawing on the front of the envelope that this dress is made like an apron? It has a front, a back and a neckhole, and is joined only at the shoulders.

Seeing the line drawings really helps us to understand what the details on a garment are, where the darts are, if there is gathering, where the zip is placed (if there is one) and so on, and this can influence our pattern choice. So look closely at the line drawings before finally making your purchase. You can do this online too, if you are buying your patterns that way.

## Pattern Body Measurements

The pattern measurements seen in Fig. 5 are overlooked by many of us. They are often on the flap of the envelope or placed above the fabric requirements, but sometimes we have to search them out.

These standard body measurements are very important because they are the actual body measurements that the pattern house has

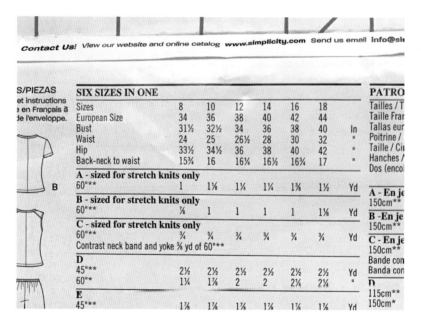

Contact Us! View our website and online catalog www.simplicity.com Send us email info@si...

| SIX SIZES IN ONE | | | | | | | | |
|---|---|---|---|---|---|---|---|---|
| Sizes | 8 | 10 | 12 | 14 | 16 | 18 | | |
| European Size | 34 | 36 | 38 | 40 | 42 | 44 | | |
| Bust | 31½ | 32½ | 34 | 36 | 38 | 40 | In | |
| Waist | 24 | 25 | 26½ | 28 | 30 | 32 | " | |
| Hip | 33½ | 34½ | 36 | 38 | 40 | 42 | " | |
| Back-neck to waist | 15¾ | 16 | 16¼ | 16½ | 16¾ | 17 | " | |
| **A - sized for stretch knits only** | | | | | | | | |
| 60"** | 1 | 1⅛ | 1¼ | 1¼ | 1⅜ | 1½ | Yd | |
| **B - sized for stretch knits only** | | | | | | | | |
| 60"** | ⅞ | 1 | 1 | 1 | 1 | 1⅛ | Yd | |
| **C - sized for stretch knits only** | | | | | | | | |
| 60"** | ¾ | ¾ | ¾ | ¾ | ¾ | ¾ | Yd | |
| Contrast neck band and yoke ⅜ yd of 60"** | | | | | | | | |
| **D** | | | | | | | | |
| 45"** | 2½ | 2½ | 2½ | 2½ | 2½ | 2½ | Yd | |
| 60"* | 1¼ | 1⅜ | 2 | 2 | 2¼ | 2¼ | " | |
| **E** | | | | | | | | |
| 45"** | 1⅞ | 1⅞ | 1⅞ | 1⅞ | 1⅞ | 1⅞ | Yd | |

S/PIEZAS
et instructions
e en Français à
de l'enveloppe.

PATRO
Tailles / T
Taille Frar
Tallas eur
Poitrine /
Taille / Ci
Hanches /
Dos (encol

A - En je
150cm**
B -En je
150cm**
C - En je
150cm**
Bande con
Banda con
D
115cm**
150cm*

**Fig. 5   Standard body measurements used to draft the pattern design.**

used to draft and make the pattern. Some of the established pattern houses still use measurements quite close to those they used a long time ago when patterns were first produced

commercially, and as a result they don't fit the modern shape of women as well as they could. So what often happens is that our personal measurements regularly cross over two or sometimes even three sizes. We'll address how to solve this in the next chapter.

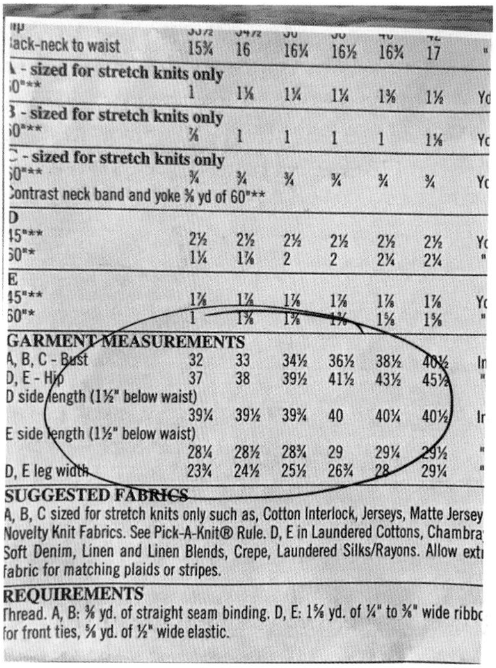

## Finished Garment Measurements

Finished garment measurements are extremely useful – when we can find them! They are often found at the bottom of the back of the envelope (see Fig. 6). They tell us what the actual finished size of key measurements (bust, waist, hips, length) of the garment will be. Not all of these measurements will be included on the pattern envelope, and some that we would like to see are often not shown. Many pattern houses are now printing finished bust and hip measurements on the pattern pieces, and although not nearly so handy, you might be able to find the information there.

Once we have found the finished garment measurements, we use them to help us understand whether the garment is close-fitting or

| | | | | | | | |
|---|---|---|---|---|---|---|---|
| ip | 33½ | 34½ | 36 | 38 | 40 | 42 | |
| Back-neck to waist | 15¾ | 16 | 16¼ | 16½ | 16¾ | 17 | " |
| **A - sized for stretch knits only** | | | | | | | |
| 60"** | 1 | 1⅛ | 1¼ | 1¼ | 1⅜ | 1½ | Yd |
| **B - sized for stretch knits only** | | | | | | | |
| 60"** | ⅞ | 1 | 1 | 1 | 1 | 1⅛ | Yd |
| **C - sized for stretch knits only** | | | | | | | |
| 60"** | ¾ | ¾ | ¾ | ¾ | ¾ | ¾ | Yd |
| Contrast neck band and yoke ⅜ yd of 60"** | | | | | | | |
| **D** | | | | | | | |
| 45"** | 2½ | 2½ | 2½ | 2½ | 2½ | 2½ | Yd |
| 60"* | 1¼ | 1⅜ | 2 | 2 | 2¼ | 2¼ | " |
| **E** | | | | | | | |
| 45"** | 1⅞ | 1¼ | 1¼ | 1⅞ | 1⅞ | 1⅞ | Yd |
| 60"* | 1 | 1⅜ | 1⅜ | 1⅜ | 1⅜ | 1⅜ | " |
| **GARMENT MEASUREMENTS** | | | | | | | |
| A, B, C - Bust | 32 | 33 | 34½ | 36½ | 38½ | 40½ | In |
| D, E - Hip | 37 | 38 | 39½ | 41½ | 43½ | 45½ | " |
| D side length (1½" below waist) | | | | | | | |
| | 39½ | 39½ | 39¾ | 40 | 40¼ | 40½ | In |
| E side length (1½" below waist) | | | | | | | |
| | 28¼ | 28½ | 28¾ | 29 | 29¼ | 29½ | " |
| D, E leg width | 23¾ | 24½ | 25¼ | 26¾ | 28 | 29¼ | " |

**SUGGESTED FABRICS**

A, B, C sized for stretch knits only such as, Cotton Interlock, Jerseys, Matte Jersey Novelty Knit Fabrics. See Pick-A-Knit® Rule. D, E in Laundered Cottons, Chambra Soft Denim, Linen and Linen Blends, Crepe, Laundered Silks/Rayons. Allow ext fabric for matching plaids or stripes.

**REQUIREMENTS**

Thread. A, B: ⅝ yd. of straight seam binding. D, E: 1⅝ yd. of ¼" to ⅜" wide ribbc for front ties, ⅝ yd. of ½" wide elastic.

**Fig. 6   Actual measurements when the garment is made up and ready to wear.**

has lots of wearing ease, and/or what the final length of each option will be.

How we do this is by comparing the finished garment measurements with the body measurements that we have just looked at, size by size. So, if the finished bust measurement of a size 14 dress is very close to the size 14 body measurements, then we know that the dress is going to be close-fitting. Conversely, if the finished garment measurements are quite a bit larger than the body measurements, then the garment is clearly a looser-fitting garment and has much more wearing ease included. This might have been clear from the picture on the front of the pattern envelope and from the line drawings, but it is very useful to check the finished measurements just to make sure that we choose the right size of pattern to cut out and sew to get a finished garment that suits us.

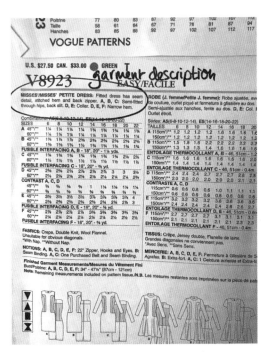

Fig. 7   Description of the garment indicating the fit and fastenings.

## Garment Description and Ease

There is always a short paragraph describing the garment on your pattern envelope (*see* Fig. 7). The description should tell you if the garment is close-fitting or loose-fitting, whether it has princess seams, side zip, front pockets and so on. If you have compared the finished garment measurements with the pattern body measurements, go on to read the garment description and it should confirm what you have learned from the measurements.

All garments have some ease in them, except for fully stretch garments such as swimwear, gym wear and dance wear, where the garments stretch onto the body for a body-contouring fit. Ease is about how much movement you get in a garment. Normal wearing ease means that although a garment fits you neatly, you can still move in it; you can sit, walk and raise your arms. A good amount of wearing ease for a close-fitting garment would be almost 5cm or 2in around the bust and hips.

Design ease is the amount of fabric needed to create the style of the garment and can be much more than 5cm/2in around the bust and hips. For instance, a loose, flowing top or dress might have several extra centimetres/inches of ease included because that is what the designer intended for the garment.

Ease is important in a pattern design because it is what makes a garment 'wearable'. It is also quite useful, because if you decide that you don't want quite so much ease in your garment, you can sometimes drop a size when you are cutting out your pattern pieces and make your garment closer-fitting. However, beware! Always measure and check. Once your fabric is cut, it can't be made bigger.

## Fabric Suggestion and Notions

Suggested fabrics for making the garment are always included on the back of the pattern envelope. In Fig. 7 you can see that fabric suggestions and notions are listed just below the fabric requirements.

It is always wise to heed the fabric suggestions, particularly if you are inexperienced or new to sewing, and particularly because today we have so many amazing fabrics that all sew very differently. Many designs are made specifically for stable fabrics, that is fabrics without any stretch in them. But others are designed for stretch fabrics only. If you decide to make a stretch pattern with a stable fabric, you could end up with some very tricky fitting problems for two reasons. First, a pattern designed for a stretch fabric is usually slightly smaller-fitting than one for a stable fabric. Also, it is unlikely to have darts or other stitched fitting features because, being a stretch fabric, it doesn't need them as the fitting happens when the garment stretches over your body. Conversely, if you choose a stretch fabric for a pattern recommended for a stable fabric, it is likely to be too big, because a pattern designed for a stable fabric has to have wearing ease built into it for fitting comfort.

Notions is a funny word, and is traditionally used to mean the things you will need to finish your garment. These are zips (and the required length will be clearly stated), buttons, elastic, thread, shoulder pads, buckles and so on. It's always a good idea to buy your thread and zip at least when you buy your fabric. Then you know that when you're ready to sew, you have everything to hand. Buttons, buckles and so on can be bought later, as it may be that you're not sure how you want to finish your garment until it's nearly completed. Buttons and other embellishments can become a design statement, so choose carefully and be creative.

## Stretch Guide

If your pattern is designed for a stretch fabric,

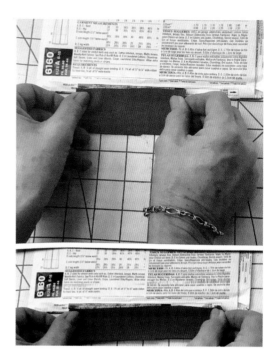

**Fig. 8   Using the stretch guide.**

you'll find a stretch guide, usually along the side of the pattern envelope (see Fig. 8). This is to help you choose the right type of stretch fabric, as there are many degrees of stretch in fabric. Some fabrics have two-way stretch, and others have just one-way stretch. Some fabrics have a huge amount of stretch, like dance-wear fabrics and T-shirt fabrics, but other fabrics, like Ponte jersey, have a much smaller amount of stretch. Most bolts of fabric are labelled and should give you an indication of the percentage of stretch included in the weave. You can feel the stretch in many fabrics and shop staff should also be able to advise.

Once you have chosen your fabric, take a small length of the fabric (as noted on the guide) and stretch it to the end of the stretch guide. If it doesn't reach, then there is not enough stretch in the fabric for the garment, and therefore it might not look or fit quite as designed. If it exceeds the guide by a lot, there could be too much stretch in the fabric. This may cause the garment not to fit as intended and the final garment may droop, or it may drop or stretch over time. The stretch guide is a very useful tool if you are new to using stretch fabrics and you need some guidance as to the suitability of your chosen fabric for the top or dress you want to make.

## Fabric Requirements

This is the part of the envelope that we are all familiar with and that we normally go to first! How much fabric do we need to buy to make this garment? Again, follow the guide, and buy your lining fabric at the same time, if required.

## Inside the Envelope

When you open your pattern, you will find two separate items: one is the instruction sheet(s) and the other is the pattern itself. The instruction sheet contains every bit of information that you will need to make your garment. It should enable anyone to sew a garment from start to finish. However, those of us who sew regularly know that pattern instruction sheets aren't always that easy to understand!

## The Instruction Sheet

### Line Drawings and Pattern Pieces

The first thing you will see on the top left-hand corner of page 1 of the instruction sheet shown in Fig. 9 is another set of line drawings of the garment(s) included in the pattern. Below or beside that, you should see a diagram of each pattern piece included in the envelope. All the pieces will be numbered, and below them you will find a numbered list, naming each piece: for example, skirt front, skirt back, skirt facing or

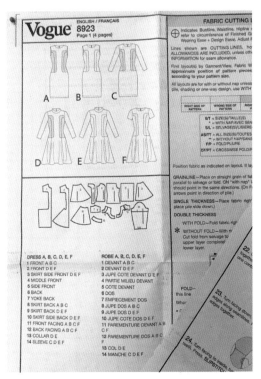

**Fig. 9 Example of an instruction sheet included in a pattern envelope.**

skirt waistband, bodice front, side front bodice, bodice back, side back bodice and so on.

In a pattern with many different design options, the line drawings will be labelled A, B, C, D and so on. This shows all the different options you can make. For instance, the garment might have options for sleeves (different sleeve styles or sleeveless), necklines (round neck or V neck) and lengths (long, knee-length or short). The pattern pieces will also be labelled accordingly. Choose your design option and note the alphabetical label it has been given. Then go to the list of pattern pieces and look for every piece that has your option letter against it. Put a little mark beside each piece with a pen or pencil and this will become your checklist for your pattern pieces. This will help to ensure that you don't end up cutting pieces you don't need, or that you forget to cut pieces that you will need.

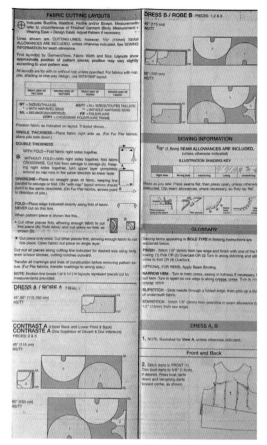

**Fig. 10 Sewing techniques included on the instruction sheet.**

## Sewing Information

Looking across the instruction sheet (*see* Fig. 10), you will find a section that will explain the sewing techniques that are required for construction of the garment. There should be a note of the seam allowance, which is normally 1.5cm or 5/8in, seam finishing techniques such as zigzagging, binding or overlocking/serging raw edges, buttonhole instructions, zip insertion instructions and so on.

These instructions can be a bit daunting, so if you are an inexperienced sewer, don't panic if you can't understand them! There are lots of ways of learning how to sew, and one of the best ways is not to rush and take each sewing step one at a time.

## Pattern Layout

A layout for cutting out your pattern is also included on your instruction sheet (*see* Fig. 10). Laying out your pattern pieces on your fabric is quite straightforward if you follow some simple rules. Just remember always to make sure that your fabric is folded on the straight grain, unless specifically instructed differently. Lay all your pattern pieces on your fabric before you begin pinning them to the fabric. This way you will know immediately if you have enough fabric, and you may also be able to lay your pattern pieces a little more sensibly or economically than the pattern instruction sheet suggests.

All pattern pieces must be laid on the fabric according to their grain instructions, with pieces that must be cut on the fold placed directly on the fold of the fabric. Finally, if your fabric has a one-way pattern, make very sure that all pattern pieces are running in the same direction, that is with the top of the pattern pieces all lying the same way on the fabric. The last thing you want is to cut everything out beautifully, only to find you have cut one of the pieces upside down!

Again, for new sewers, understanding the pattern layout can take a bit of time, but full instructions are given on the sheet.

## Sewing Instructions

To make your garment successfully, it is very important to sew everything in the right order. The sewing instructions give you step-by-step numbered instructions, both in drawings and writing, telling you how to make your garment (*see* Fig. 11). Many of us struggle with understanding the written instructions, so it is often much easier to 'read' the pictures first. Look at each diagram and work out what you have to do at that stage. Once you think you have worked it out, then check the narrative to see if it agrees with your assessment of what you should be doing, and you should find that the instructions are much easier to follow.

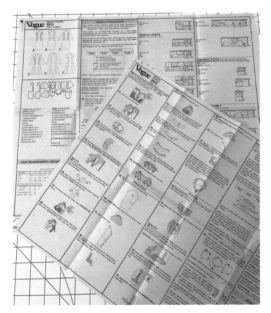

**Fig. 11  Step-by-step sewing instructions in pictures and words.**

The sewing instructions will take you from the very first sewing step, after cutting out your pieces in fabric, to the final finishing steps needed to complete your garment. Just remember that some patterns have several design options included, and it may be that you are making garment C out of options A, B and C. Some instructions may be for garments A and B only, so be careful to note which instructions pertain to your pattern option.

The more you sew and use different patterns, the easier it will be to understand the instruction sheets, and this is because your sewing experience will begin to tell you how certain pieces should be stitched together.

## Pattern Pieces

Now we come to the exciting bit, the pattern pieces themselves. All commercial patterns today are multi-size. That means that they include pattern pieces sized from, for example,

6 to 14 (UK sizes) and then 14 to 22 (UK sizes). Each pattern piece has clear information printed on it, including the pattern design number (for example, Simplicity 1234, Vogue 9876 and so on), the pattern piece number and the name of the piece (for example, side front panel, trouser front, side facing and so on). This information will also tell you whether the piece should be cut on the fold and how many pieces you should cut in fabric, lining and/or interfacing.

Fig. 12 shows just one pattern piece before it is cut out of the whole pattern tissue. You can see the pattern number at the top of the pattern piece, followed by the name of the piece (Front – A, B). Just below that we are told how many pieces of fabric and/or lining to cut. This pattern piece has to be cut on the fold of the fabric. This means that the pattern piece has to be laid directly on the fold of the fabric and the long line with arrowheads at each end,

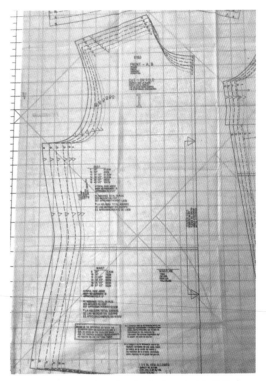

**Fig. 12  A multi-size pattern piece with full cutting instructions and sewing guides marked.**

down the right-hand side of the pattern piece, shows us clearly which side has to go against the fold of the fabric. There should also be an instruction along this line telling you to place the pattern piece on the fold of the fabric. Whenever this style of line is drawn on a pattern piece, it indicates that the piece must be cut on the fold of the fabric, even if no instruction is written against this line.

> **Note:** a pattern piece is laid on the fold of the fabric because there will be no seams down the centre of that piece of the garment. So when the piece is cut and opened up, it fits right across the body and seams will be at the side of the garment only.

Moving down the pattern piece, we can see that bust measurements are stated, together with a note of the bust ease that is included in this pattern. The waistline is also marked, making it easier for us to understand before we cut whether the pattern is going to be too long, too short or just right for us in terms of body length. Finally, at the bottom of the pattern piece the hem allowance is clearly marked.

As commercial patterns are multi-sized, each pattern piece has several cutting lines. Each cutting line will be labelled with a different size and some patterns will have different ways of marking the lines for each size. So you may find dotted, dashed or solid lines for each of the different sizes. The different sizes can be seen marked on the left-hand side of the pattern in Fig. 13.

Once you have decided which size you should cut, then carefully cut along the size line you have chosen. It is very important to cut absolutely on that line. If you cut outside or inside that line, you will be cutting your pattern either too big or too small. You will be changing your seam allowance and therefore the garment will not be true for fitting purposes.

Many patterns will have the same pattern piece printed twice or even three times on the pattern tissue. Look carefully at the sizing, because each of these pieces will be for different sizes and/or different cup sizes. Make sure you choose the correct piece for the size you are cutting.

The symbols or notations included on a pattern piece can cause some confusion. All the symbols on a pattern piece have a purpose, and it helps with sewing a successful garment if we take note of and use that information.

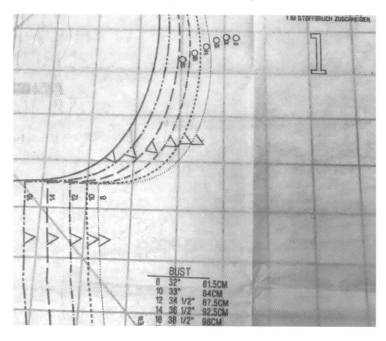

Fig. 13  **Multi-size cutting lines on a pattern piece.**

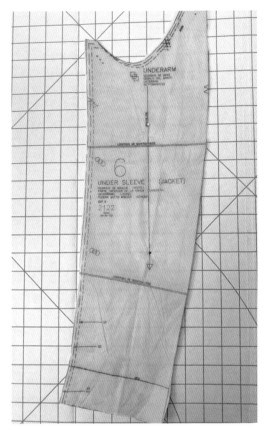

**Fig. 14  Notches on a pattern piece, used for matching when sewing.**

**Note:** the grainline always runs parallel to the selvedge of your fabric. If your fabric is folded neatly, with opposite selvedges together, you can use the selvedge as a guide to see if you have placed your pattern pieces on the grainline. Measure the distance between the grainline and the selvedge at both ends of the grainline. So long as the measurement out to the selvedge is the same at both ends of the grainline, your pattern piece will be lying straight on the grainline.

## Grainline

This is the first mark to take note of. It is critical, for fit, drape and sewing purposes, to ensure that your pattern piece follows the grainline instruction when you place it on the fabric, regardless of how you think it could be placed. If you don't follow the grainline instructions on your pattern pieces, after you have cut the pieces and begin to sew them together, you might find that the fabric pieces don't go

**Fig. 15  Pitch points – small circles often found at the armhole to help with altering the size of the pattern.**

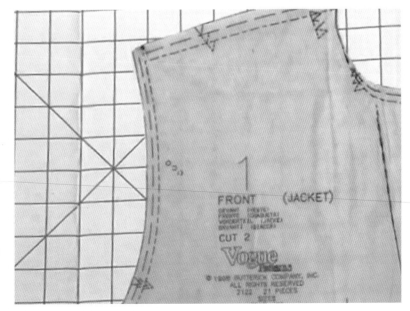

together very well. This is because you have cut your pattern pieces slightly on the bias or cross grain, and this can cause the fabric pieces to stretch out of shape when sewing, and even worse, when wearing the garment.

In Fig. 14 the grainline can be seen clearly, running down the centre of the pattern piece. It is a straight line with an arrowhead at each end.

## Notches

These are marked as small triangles on the cutting lines of each piece. They are important for matching pieces when sewing your garment together In Fig. 14 the notches can be seen on the upper side edges of the pattern piece. There are two notches on the right-hand seam and one on the left-hand seam.

## Pitch Points

These are little standalone circles that you might see close to the armhole or possibly near the crotch seam on trousers. They are mostly a pattern-drafting notation and will be used if a significant alteration has been made that requires the armhole or other curve to be redrafted. Most of us don't use them and they needn't be transferred onto your fabric.

## Lengthen and Shorten Lines

These are closely placed double lines and will be marked with the words 'lengthen or shorten here'. You can see examples in Figs 14 and 16. Fig. 14 has two sets of lengthen/shorten lines, one above the elbow and one below the elbow. Fig. 16 has one set of lengthen/ shorten lines near the waistline. They are placed on the garment to allow length alterations to be made without affecting the overall style and design of the garment. Sometimes we might choose to lengthen or shorten at the hem of a garment, but that can often change the line of a garment, for example by making a flared skirt or boot-leg trousers either too full or too narrow at the hem.

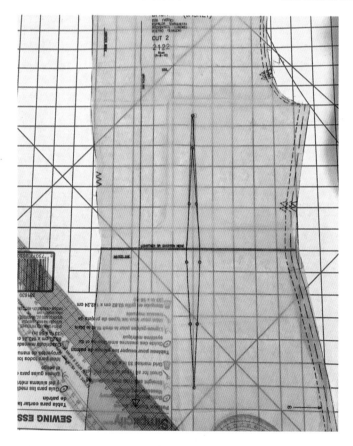

## Darts

These are critical for sewing because they give shape to most

**Fig. 16   Lengthen and shorten lines for adjusting the length of the pattern.**

**Fig. 17 Single-ended darts marked in multiple sizes.**

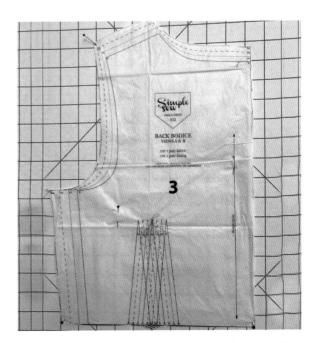

of the garments that we make. Darts can be both single- and double-ended. Single-ended darts are used for bust and waist fitting, and double-ended darts are most often used for body shaping from below the bust down towards the hips. Darts are marked with small circles and straight lines running into and through the circles.

You can see examples of both single- and double-ended darts in Figs 17 and 18. The single-ended dart has multi-size options included, so it's important to choose the correct dart to mark and sew. The double-ended dart in Fig. 18 is one size only on this particular pattern. However, a double-ended dart can also have different size options, so again, it is very important to make sure that the correct size is marked properly before sewing, otherwise it could end up being in the wrong place.

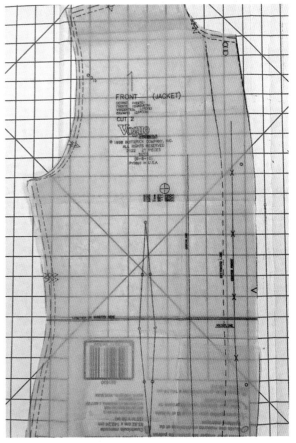

**Fig. 18 Double-ended dart in one size only.**

Bust
Point

High bust

Bust

Waist

Hips

# UNDERSTANDING YOUR BODY MEASUREMENTS

You might ask why you need to understand your personal body measurements. You might think you know them. After all, you know your bra size and your dress size. Are there any more measurements that you need?

Commercial patterns are made to a standard size using standard body measurements as set by the pattern houses. However, we all know that none of us is a standard size. The smallest and the tallest, the thinnest and the cuddliest of us are not a standard size. Therefore, it's important and very useful to understand our personal body measurements, because they help us to understand our personal body shape, whether we like it or not. But more than that, they help us to understand why certain garments don't fit in the way we'd like and why other garments work really well for us. They can help us to choose the best styles to wear and can indicate what we should avoid in both home-created and ready-to-wear clothing.

## Understanding Personal Body Measurements

For most home sewers, there are some key body measurements that we must take note of. These include high bust, bust, waist, hips, high hips, bust point and back length. Many diagrams describing body measurements often include a lot of other measurements too. These other measurements are predominantly needed for pattern drafting – creating personal patterns from scratch – and will include the measurement around the armhole (armscye), the measurement around the neck, arm lengths, bicep measurements and so on. For the majority of home sewers, these are areas of fitting that can be altered during the fitting process if required. For those of us who are able to draft our own patterns, these extra measurements will be very important.

## Key Body Measurements

Figs 19, 20 and 21 explain the key body measurements that all home sewers should understand. These are marked with red lines in the diagrams.

1. **High bust** – this measurement is taken directly under the arms and above the bust. The tape must be straight across the back. It is this measurement subtracted from the bust measurement that helps us to understand cup size.

2. **Full bust** – taken directly over the fullest part of the bust, again keeping the tape as straight as possible across the back.

3. **Front chest** – this measurement is taken from armhole side seam to armhole side

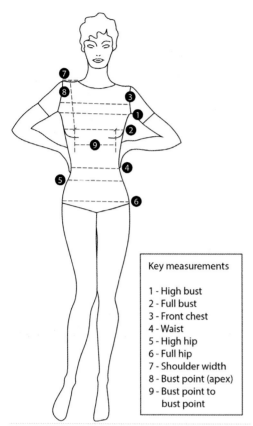

**Key measurements**

1 - High bust
2 - Full bust
3 - Front chest
4 - Waist
5 - High hip
6 - Full hip
7 - Shoulder width
8 - Bust point (apex)
9 - Bust point to
     bust point

Fig. 19   Body measurement diagram – front.

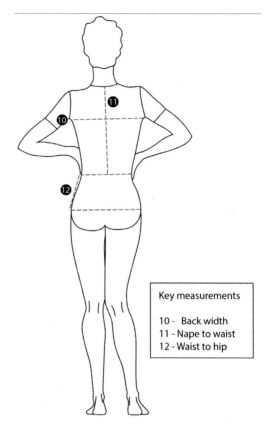

**Key measurements**

10 -  Back width
11 - Nape to waist
12 - Waist to hip

Fig. 20   Body measurement diagram – back.

seam across the front of the body and will not necessarily be half the bust measurement.

4.   **Waist** – this is the narrowest part of the body, not where you choose to wear your skirts or trousers. The best way to find your natural waist is to tie a narrow piece of elastic around your middle. It should naturally move to the narrowest part of the torso and denote the waist (about level with your belly button). It might seem very high compared to where you think your waist is, but that is the measurement used by the pattern houses.

5.   **High hip** – this is approximately 10cm/4in below the waist (leave your piece of elastic in place) and allows us to understand

how the tummy will impact the fit of our clothes.

6.   **Full hip** – this is approximately 20–22cm/8–9in below the waist. Make sure that the measurement is taken at the fullest part of the hip – it helps if you try and locate the hip bone to ensure you are measuring in the correct place.

7.   **Shoulder width** – measure along a natural seam line from the side of the neck to the tip of the shoulder. The standard measurement is 10cm/4in. If it helps, try to locate where the shoulder 'hinges', or think of the shoulder tip as where a sleeve seam would lie on a well-fitting shirt.

8.   **Bust point (apex)** – this measures to the apex of the bust from the centre of

the shoulder. A standard measurement is about 22cm/9in, but many of us vary from this, particularly those with a fuller bust, where the measurement may be greater than the standard.

9. **Bust point to bust point (apex to apex)** – this is the distance between the bust points. If this measurement is quite large, then darts may have to be shortened slightly, or moved to the left, to ensure they are not finishing on the bust point.

10. **Back width** – this is taken from one armhole side seam to the other across the back and approximately 10cm/4in below the nape of the neck. This measurement will clarify if your back is broader or narrower than the standard measurement.

11. **Nape to waist** – if you are wearing a neckchain, the nape is where the chain naturally rests on the back of your neck. Measure from here to your piece of elastic or your natural waist. Most commercial patterns set this measurement at 40cm/16in, so it's important to know if you have a shorter or longer back length than allowed for in the pattern.

12. **Waist to hip** – using your piece of elastic as your guide, measure from here to your hip. Again, it helps a great deal to know if the pattern standard measurement suits you or if it might need to be lengthened or shortened.

13. **Crotch depth or rise** – this measurement is taken sitting on a flat surface and measuring from the waist to the flat surface. This measurement allows us to achieve better fitting for trousers.

The following set of measurements are those used for pattern drafting. We don't normally have to worry about these, because we can mostly deal with them when we are fitting a garment.

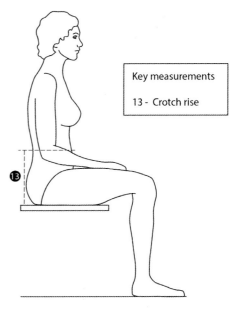

Key measurements

13 - Crotch rise

**Fig. 21   Body measurement diagram – trousers.**

- Neck
- Bicep
- Wrist
- Armhole/armscye
- Shoulder to elbow
- Elbow to wrist
- Thigh
- Calf
- Waist to knee
- Waist to floor – right
- Waist to floor – left

# Choosing the Right Size of Pattern to Cut

Now that we have a clear picture of our personal body measurements and shape, we can go back to our pattern envelope. We look at the pattern measurements on the back of the envelope and we match our measurements to them. As often as not, our measurements will cross two, and sometimes three pattern sizes. So how do we choose which size to cut? The rule is that if you are going to make a garment that hangs from the shoulders, such as a dress or a top, you use your bust measurement as your guide size. If you are making a garment that hangs from the waist, such as trousers or a skirt, you use your hip measurement as your guide size.

## TIP: CHOOSING THE RIGHT SIZE PATTERN

It is much easier to cut a larger size pattern, and reduce it to make it fit better, than it is to cut a smaller size and have to size it up. It's very tricky for most of us to size a pattern up more than one or two sizes. It's much easier to make our pattern smaller in the areas we need to adjust.

## Cutting to Fit Bust Size

It is important to understand the relationship between bust measurements and sizing. Cup size for purchased underwear does not relate to cup size in sewing patterns. All commercial patterns are made to a standard B cup measurement, but most ladies are not a standard B cup size. This is how to calculate your cup size for home sewing.

First, measure your high bust and take a note of the measurement. Then measure your actual bust and subtract your high bust measurement from that. The number you are left with will denote your cup size for making your own clothes. See the cup size calculator table for help in understanding your cup size. Remember – it is *not* the same as the cup size you buy in commercially made underwear!

Unless your pattern has optional cup sizes included, in which case you can cut the appropriate pattern piece for your bust measurement,

## CUP SIZE CALCULATOR

A cup = 2.5cm/1in or less
B cup = 2.5–5cm/1–2in
C cup = 5–7.5cm/2–3in
D cup = 7.5–10cm/3–4in
DD cup = 10–12.5cm/4–5in
DDD cup = 12.5–15cm/5–6in

then it will be important to choose the bust size carefully before you cut your pattern tissue. This is how to decide which size is right for you:

- A or B cup – if you measure as an A or a B cup, cut the pattern piece according to your bust measurement and then make any adjustments, if required, on the toile.
- C cup or larger – if you measure as a C cup or larger, you should use your *high bust* measurement to choose which pattern size to cut, and then make a full bust adjustment after the first fitting. If you don't do this and you use your actual bust measurement, you will find that your garment will almost certainly be too big around the armhole and on the shoulders. This is because the whole pattern is designed for a much bigger person and not for someone with only a fuller bust.

Whether you have a small or full bust, you must also take into account your tummy and buttocks. If they are also fuller, then measure your pattern piece around the waist and tummy area to make sure it will fit. If it is going to be too close-fitting, cut a larger size on that part of the pattern piece.

## Cutting to Fit Tummy and Hips

You may find that your high hip measurement (around the tummy) is bigger than your hip measurement. If this is the case and you are making trousers or a skirt, then use the high hip measurement as your size guide for cutting out your pattern pieces. This will ensure a better fit across the tummy for both skirts and trousers.

## Cutting Across Different Sizes on Your Pattern Pieces

Multi-sizing on a pattern allows for other cutting considerations, too. If you realize from your personal measurements that you are a combination of sizes, then the pattern can be cut in the combination that suits you best. For instance, if you have a narrow back and a fuller front, then cut the back in a smaller size and the front in the size that you have decided you need. Your hips may be narrow in comparison to your waist, so it's a good idea to cut the waist in the size you need and graduate to the smaller size around the hips. Conversely, if you need more room around the hips and less on the waist, then graduate from the cutting line at the hips to a smaller one at the waist. This will make for a pattern that is immediately more

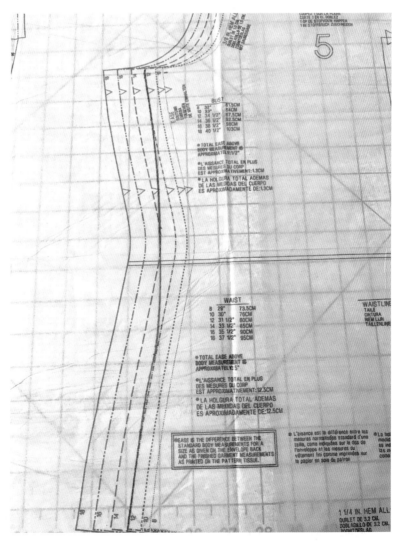

**Fig. 22  Cutting across different size lines to increase the waist.**

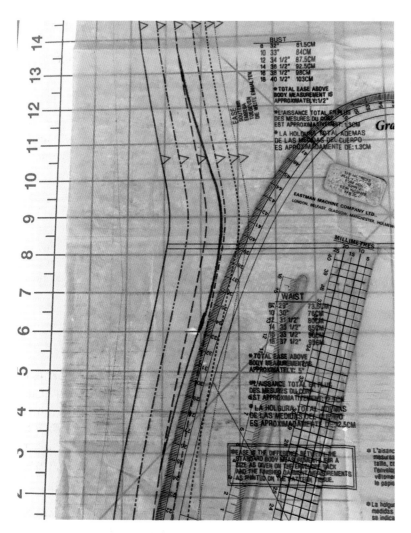

**Fig. 23  Cutting across different size lines to reduce the waist.**

suited to your personal body shape. Figs 22 and 23 show how moving from one cutting line to another is quite straightforward and can make a significant difference to the overall fit.

In Fig. 22, a red line has been drawn from one size at the bust to the next size up at the waist and then back again to the original smaller size at the hip. This will increase the waist size for a more comfortable fit. In Fig. 23, the opposite has been done. The waist measurement has been reduced for a better fit.

Both alterations shown in Figs 22 and 23 have been made with the French curve to ensure a smooth transition from one cutting line to the next and back. They have also been made before the pattern tissue has been cut. These simple alterations can be done in a variety of places on the pattern tissue before any cutting is started. For instance, if you know you have narrow shoulders and always have to alter them, then cut a smaller size at the shoulder and graduate to the appropriate size for the rest of the armhole (see Fig. 24). If you always have to increase or decrease the waist size on a skirt or trouser pattern, then make the alteration on the pattern tissue before you cut it. However, just to be sure, *always* check the measurements before you cut!

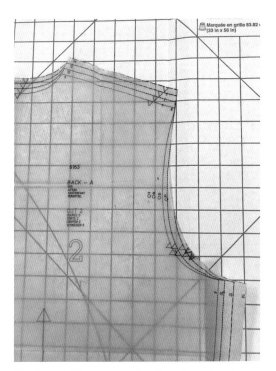

**Fig. 24   Cutting across size lines to make the shoulder slightly narrower.**

You are now finally ready to cut and sew your toile!

## Cutting Out

There are some key points to remember for successful cutting out. If you cut your pattern

### TIP: SIZE IS JUST A NUMBER!

Remember: the size we cut and sew for home-created garments is almost always at least one, if not two sizes bigger than we buy in ready-to-wear!

### TIPS: PREPARING YOUR PATTERN

- Always cut your pattern out exactly on the size line that you have chosen. Don't leave a margin around the edge, because this will use extra fabric when laying your pattern out and it may cause you to cut the wrong size.
- Iron your pattern pieces with a cool iron if they are creased. This helps you to lay them out properly.
- Keep larger pieces of waste pattern tissue to one side. They come in very handy when making pattern alterations.

and fabric as accurately as possible, your fabric pieces will match perfectly, so you will ultimately sew more accurate seams and have more accurate seam allowances. Take some time to lay your pattern out carefully before cutting and use your best cutting scissors. The following tips should help:

**Lay *all* your pattern pieces on the fabric before pinning and cutting.** Move them around to get the best from your piece of fabric, remembering always to follow grainline instructions. This will ensure that you have enough fabric to cut out all your pieces.

**Pin the grainline first.** This will keep the pattern piece from moving out of alignment whilst you pin around the edges.

**Place your pins slightly in from the edge of the pattern tissue**, but not too far in that the edge of the pattern lifts when you are cutting. If you pin very close to the edge of the pattern and use a lot of pins, they can actually hinder your smooth cutting and get in the way of the scissors.

**Flip your pattern pieces over if it helps them to fit on your fabric better.** Not all your pattern pieces need to lie face up on the fabric. You can flip them over, so that you are looking at the back or reverse of the pattern piece, if it helps them to fit on your fabric better, as you will still get two mirror image pieces to sew.

**Always check how many fabric pieces you have to cut.** Some pattern pieces only require one fabric piece to be cut (for example, an asymmetric top or dress) and therefore don't need to be cut on folded (double) fabric.

**Always cut as close to the edge of your paper pattern as you can.** Any deviation, either outside or inside the cutting line, will change the size and therefore the fit of your final garment.

**Cut flat on your cutting surface.** In other words, don't lift your fabric with the pattern pinned on it, otherwise your cutting will not be accurate.

## Preparing to Sew

It is almost time to sew your toile! However, there are some essential things to do before you begin sewing, including transferring your notches to your fabric and also marking darts, buttonholes, zip placements and so on, on your fabric.

### Notches

These are the little triangles that appear along the cutting lines of the pattern pieces and are used to make sure that we match our fabric pieces correctly before sewing. There are several ways of marking these notches on our fabric pieces: one of the old-fashioned ways is to cut a triangle outwards from the cutting line into the fabric so that you can see it more

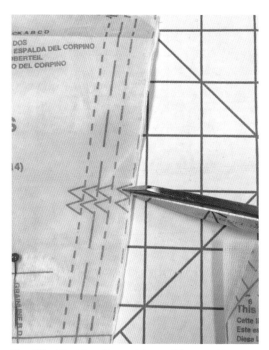

Fig. 25   **Marking the notches with a small scissor snip.**

clearly. However, this is time-consuming – and sometimes not very effective if our cutting is not as accurate as it should be, meaning that we can't see the notches very well.

A good way of marking the notches is to use only the tip of the scissors, and snip just into the triangle (and not quite to the point of the triangle). This is demonstrated in Fig. 25. It is crucial to remember to use only the tip of the scissors, otherwise you may have a disastrous cutting accident! You may worry that you will lose the notch if you overlock/serge your seams before sewing, but this is not normally the case. The notch can usually still be found even underneath an overlocked or serged edge.

### Darts

The next important job is to mark your darts. Traditionally we use a tailor's tack for this. A tailor's tack is a good and safe way to mark the position of darts without worrying about the mark disappearing. However, if you are more experienced, you can also mark darts with tailor's chalk if you know that the chalk marks won't disappear before you have time to begin sewing. To do this, you need to break through your paper pattern at the appropriate points on the dart and mark the top fabric piece with a sharp edge of chalk. To mark the second fabric piece, place your flat piece of tailor's chalk exactly underneath both pattern and fabric at the point that needs to be marked. Then, with closed scissors, rub your fabric gently to make a chalk impression underneath. This is a bit like taking a paper rubbing of a raised pattern. Check that it has worked before you move on to the next mark.

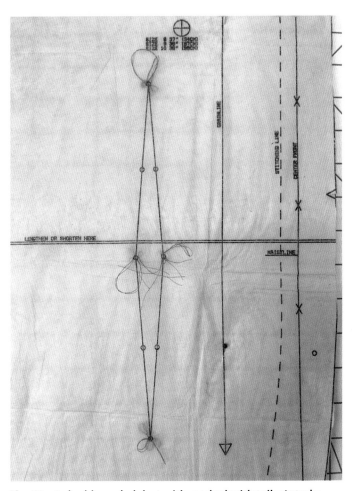

**Fig. 26  A double-ended dart with marked with tailor's tacks.**

Fig. 26 shows a double-ended dart. This dart requires marking at either end and at the widest part of the dart, and you can see from the picture that tailor's tacks have been used four times to do this. You might notice that there are also four extra matching dots along the lines of the dart. Since this dart is running pretty much in straight lines from each apex to the centre, it is not necessary to mark the extra matching dots with tailor's tacks.

Some double-ended darts are quite different in shape to the one shown in Fig. 26, and are not necessarily symmetrical down each side. If you draw a line from one end of a double-ended dart to the other, you will often find that

it is fuller on one side of your straight line, and also that the 'centre' or widest part of the dart is towards one end of the dart. In this case, it's really important to mark all the dots on the dart, because they provide the sewing line for the correct shape of the dart, and ultimately the correct fit of the dart.

Single-ended darts also have to be marked carefully to ensure their proper placement on the garment. First, it is key that the correct dart is chosen. On multi-size patterns, several darts are marked alongside each other (*see* Fig. 27), and it can be a little confusing when the lines of each dart size overlap. Mark the apex of the

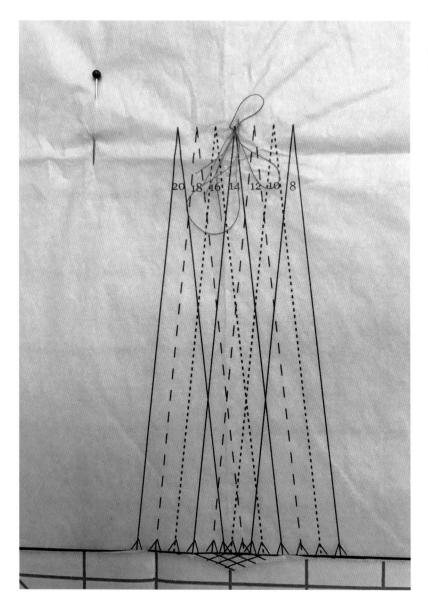

**Fig. 27   A single-ended dart with multi-size options.**

dart for the size you are sewing with a tailor's tack or chalk, and then, with your finger, trace back to the wide end of the dart at the edge of the paper pattern. When you find the first leg of the dart, mark it with the scissors in the same way as you did your pattern notches (Figs 28 and 29). Then trace the second leg of the dart and mark it in the same way.

If you have made tailor's tacks, when you are separating your pattern from your fabric before sewing, remember to hold your pattern piece in one hand very close to the tailor's tack and the tack itself in the other hand. This should ensure that the pattern doesn't tear badly and the tack doesn't come loose. You'll find a small hole in your pattern after that, so the next time you use it to make your actual garment, it will be easier to release the pattern from the fabric.

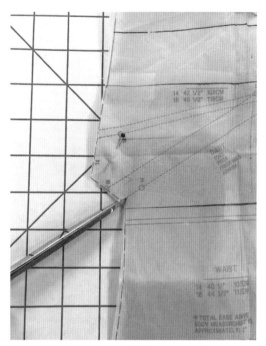

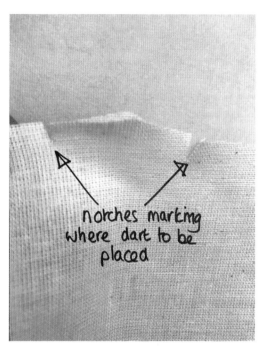

**Fig. 28  Marking the end of a dart with scissor snips.**

**Fig. 29  How the marks look on the fabric.**

## Buttonholes, Collar Placement, Zipper Placement, Pocket Placement

These will all be marked on the pattern piece with a small circle. They will not necessarily be labelled, but you will find that they correspond to the instructions given on the pattern instruction sheet. For new sewers, it is absolutely the best idea to transfer all these marks to your garment before you sew. Again, you can use tailor's tacks or chalk. More experienced sewers may know where the zipper will end and up to which point the seam needs to be sewn.

You might decide to place your buttonholes to suit your own requirements, in which case you will probably wait until you have finished making your garment before marking them, particularly if you need to make adjustments for length.

A collar placement symbol, on a blazer-type jacket for instance, will usually be found at the appropriate seam allowance cross over – that is, where the collar and the lapel meet. An experienced sewer will understand this, but a newer sewer should follow all instructions carefully and mark all collar placement symbols as given on the pattern.

Pocket placement symbols are quite important, particularly for patch pockets that will sit on top of the garment. If you don't mark the placement symbols carefully, then the pockets could end up being out of alignment.

You are now ready to cut out and sew your toile!

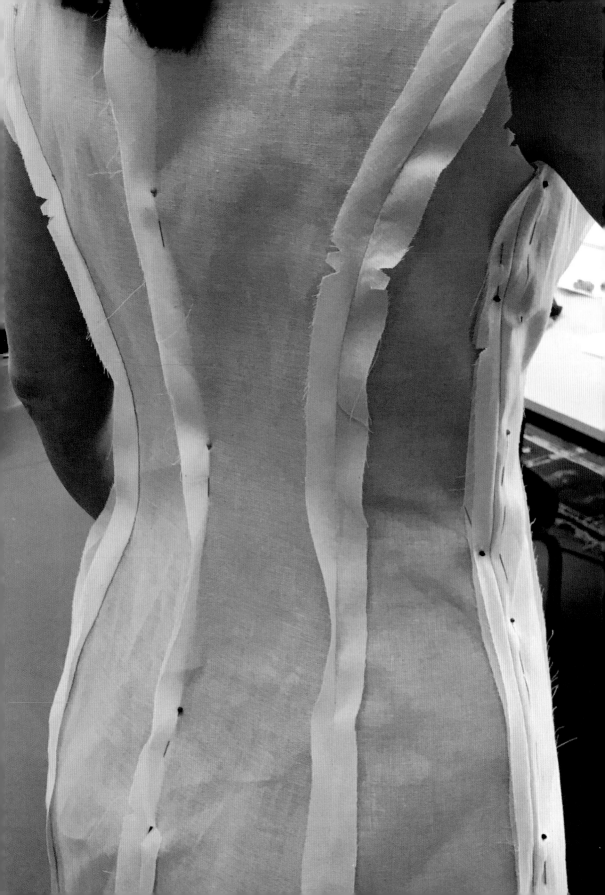

# SEWING AND FITTING THE TOILE

Making your garment twice, once in a practice fabric such as calico and then in the final fabric, may seem laborious and long-winded. All sewers want to get their garment finished and ready to wear as soon as they can. However, making a toile is the best idea for two main reasons. First, it allows a proper fitting to be done and alterations to be made to the pattern before the garment itself is cut out and stitched. Secondly, it is the best way to learn how to construct the garment before using the final fabric and possibly making errors on that. How many times have we been totally disappointed with the final outfit because it just doesn't fit well? The bust isn't quite right, or the back doesn't lie properly. Maybe it's a bit too short in the body, or the darts are not quite in the right place. You might wear the garment if the fit is just OK, but it also may go to the back of the wardrobe and never actually be worn. Making a toile removes that possibility and ultimately gives you a dress, jacket or top to be proud of.

## Fabric for the Toile

In order to make your toile, it is sensible to choose a fabric with similar characteristics to your pattern fabric requirements. If your pattern calls for a stable fabric, then calico is a very good option for making the fitting garment. Or you can use something from your stash if

you need to clear some of it out! If your pattern requires a knitted or stretch fabric, however, it is more sensible to buy an economical stretch fabric to practise on. Ideally, find a fabric that is close to what you will want to use to make the final garment, without spending a fortune on it. Many a toile has turned into a wearable garment in the end!

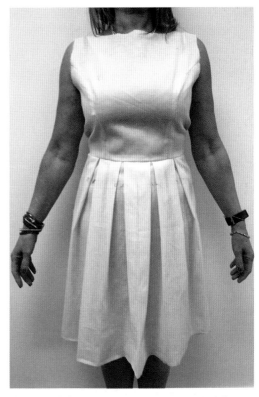

**Fig. 30  Toile of a dress made up in calico for fitting.**

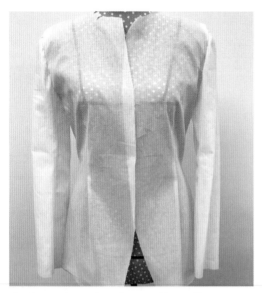

**Fig. 31  Using a dressform to fit a toile.**

## Fitting the Toile

How do you fit something on yourself? The answer is: usually, you don't. Ask a sewing friend if you need a lot of fitting help, or if you understand your own fitting requirements, ask anyone you know to help and direct them clearly in what to do with pins and a pen. Or you can use a dressform. If you do use a dressform, make sure you also try on your toile to check any fitting alterations you have made on the dressform before moving to the next stage. Working with a dressform will be illustrated later in this book.

Fitting a garment is not a precise and formulaic process. Fitting must be done on an individual basis and according to what looks good and makes the wearer feel comfortable. The same garment will have completely different fitting requirements on different people.

Fitting is usually an evolving process, especially if you are trying a new style or pattern. Sometimes it will be necessary to make up a second or even a third toile to ensure that the fit is as good as it can be, especially if a lot of alterations have been made to the original pattern. Fitting the same dress on two different people will probably entail very different fitting solutions to make the dress look really good on them both.

Fitting is a learning process, and the more you do, the more confident you will become at solving fitting problems. Fitting allows you to be creative as well, and really makes your garment a true one-off!

## How do you Recognize Fitting Problems?

When you put your toile on, there will be some very obvious fitting issues that you will see immediately. The garment may be too wide at some point on the shoulders, waist or hips, or too tight in those places. It may be pulling across the back. It may be too big or too tight across the bust. The length may be completely wrong for what you want.

There will also be some fitting issues that you might not be so aware of initially. If you try on your toile and you can see drag lines, these will indicate fitting problems too. They mean that somewhere the toile is too tight. Conversely, if your toile is too big in places, it will make the garment hang badly and not look great at all. The key thing is to understand the signs and the way in which the fabric is pulling or lying, and learn to recognize where an alteration needs to be made.

### Drag Lines

If you look at the photograph of the sleeveless dress in Fig. 32, you can see the drag lines running from the bust down to the side waist and also up to the shoulder. This is where the fabric is straining to fit and is being pulled out of shape. It is most likely due to the garment

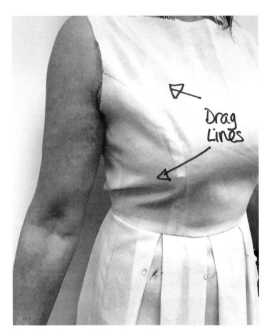

**Fig. 32 Recognising drag lines.**

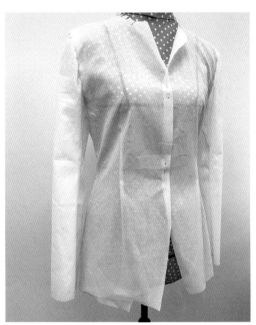

**Fig. 33 Drag lines on a jacket.**

being too tight-fitting in the bust area, causing the dress to strain across the front.

Looking at the jacket in Fig. 33, drag lines can be seen coming from the top of the bust dart down to the side waist. This jacket has a couple of buttons to close it, and it has been pinned closed on the dressform to hold it in place better. When doing this, there was no strain across the bust at all. Therefore, the drag lines are probably telling us that the jacket is too tight across the lower part of the jacket, around the upper hip, as this is where the garment is pulling back towards the side upper hip.

And if we look at the trousers in Fig. 34, the drag lines are very clear. They are running from the mid-buttocks into the inside top of the leg. The reason for this is that the crotch fitting is too close and the crotch seam is pulling up and into the model's buttocks.

These trousers are also too big across the hips, and there is excess fabric that is causing folds to appear alongside the drag lines from the centre back seam of each leg running down to below the buttocks.

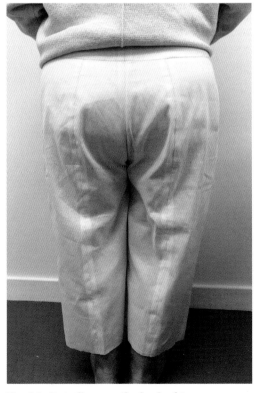

**Fig. 34 Drag lines on the back of trousers around the buttocks.**

**Fig. 35   Gaping neck and armholes on the dress.**

## Gaping Neck/Armholes

Both the neck and armholes on the dress bodice shown in Fig. 35 are gaping and the excess fabric in the neck can be seen quite clearly. It is more difficult to see the armhole gape in the dress because there is quite a lot of strain on the bodice due to the bust being too tight. However, closer examination of the toile on the wearer will show that the armhole is gaping slightly and needs to be adjusted.

## Fabric Bunching Up at the Back

In Fig. 36 we can clearly see the fabric bunching and pulling across the lower back of the dress, although the shoulders are looking OK. At first sight, it might seem that this bunching and pulling is due to the bodice being too long. However, refitting the bust (*see* Fig. 37) resulted in the dress sitting properly on the waist and only a very small length adjustment had to be made. Clearly the dress was much too tight across the front and was pulling up at the back as a result.

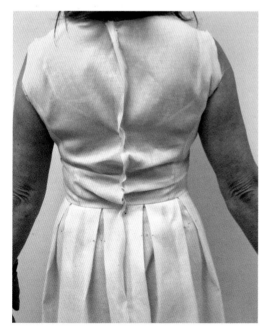

**Fig. 36   Dress back before any fitting alterations have been made.**

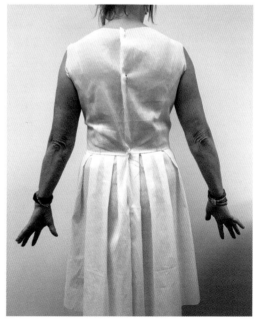

**Fig. 37   Dress back after bust-fitting alterations have been made.**

## WHAT TO LOOK FOR WHEN FITTING A TOILE

**Drag lines** – these will denote that the garment is too tight in a particular area, such as the bust, shoulders, tummy or hips.

**Gaping armholes/neck** – these are most likely due to bust-fitting problems or garment fit across the back/shoulders.

**Twisted seams** – these will probably be due to the garment being too tight somewhere.

**Fabric bunching up at the back** – this will be due to the garment being too long in the body or too tight around the middle.

**Hem rising or dipping at either front or back** – this is often due to the garment being too tight around the middle, but could also be due to a full tummy or buttocks pulling the garment up at the front or the back.

**Trouser centre back seam cutting into buttocks** – this is due to the rise being too short.

## How Do We Fix the Most Common Fitting Problems?

Probably the most common fitting problem, and the most scary, is around the bust. Darts may be in the wrong place, a princess seam may not lie correctly, or the fit at the bust is too loose or too tight.

If the fit at the bust is good, but the armhole is gaping, this means that the pattern size that has been cut is actually too big. Slight gaping can be eliminated by easing the seam with a double row of running stitches and pulling the stitches in slightly to reduce the seam line of the fabric. The pattern piece can also be darted and folded to eliminate gaping, but again only if the gaping is not significant and the pattern piece can be darted and folded without making

it too difficult to use again. Finally, darts can be made to eliminate the gaping areas if they suit the garment and the wearer, but they may not look very good and may spoil the final look of the whole garment.

The best way to avoid gaping armholes and/ or a gaping neck, neither of which look pretty or feel comfortable, is to cut a smaller pattern size based on the high bust measurement and then make a full bust adjustment (FBA). What this means is that the new garment will fit on the neck and around the armhole, but will be too small on the bust. A full bust adjustment will then need to be made, and the method for doing this is described in Chapter 4.

Fitting a small bust is not quite so daunting. If the pattern size has been chosen correctly on bust size, what might happen is that the fit at the bust is good, but the shoulders might need to be altered or the waist adjusted. These alterations are usually simpler to do, and can sometimes even be done on the tissue before the pattern piece is cut out. A small bust adjustment (SBA) on a princess seam garment is done in the same way as a full bust adjustment, except that the curve on the seam line is reduced rather than increased (*see* Chapter 4).

## Bust Darts

Bust darts are usually included in a garment first for fitting purposes, and secondly as a design feature. They mostly come from the side seam up almost to the apex of the bust, but they can also be placed from the armhole down towards the bust (although these are not so common), from the shoulder to the bust and from the waist up to the bust. So a dart can be placed where it suits and fits the wearer best, and where the designer decides it should go. Most of us will accept the dart placement as already designed on the garment, but we might have to move it to make it fit us better.

**Fig. 38 Bust dart is too high.**

**Fig. 39 Marking the toile with the new bust point/apex.**

The garment being modelled in Fig. 38 is a simple coat that does not have any fastenings. On close examination of the front of the coat, we can see that the dart is in the wrong place for this model – the model's bust apex is approximately 5cm/2in lower than the pattern. This means that the dart on this pattern is too high for this model and is not shaping the coat in the right place. The dart will need to be lowered.

### TIP: BUST DARTS

- A dart should never be long enough to reach the apex of the bust. It is much better if it comes to within about 1.5–2cm/¾in to the side and below the bust apex.
- Darts can be placed anywhere on a garment if they work for fitting and they don't spoil the look of the garment. Don't be afraid to add or remove darts if you prefer the look achieved by doing so.

**Note:** The dart on the coat in Figs. 38, 39 and 40 had to be lowered because it was too high for the wearer. But it may be that a dart is too low on a garment and will need to be lifted to make the fit better. The process for moving a dart will be described later in the book.

In Fig. 39 the toile has been turned inside out to make it easier to draw and pin alterations on the toile. It can now be seen more clearly where the model's bust apex is and therefore what point the dart should come to. The new finishing point for the dart has been marked on the toile with a black marker pen. It is important to remember that a bust dart should never come to a finishing point at the actual apex of the bust. This is not a good look! For the best look, a bust dart should typically finish slightly short of the apex and slightly below the apex by about 1.5–2cm/¾in or more.

**Fig. 40    The fit after the bust dart has been lowered.**

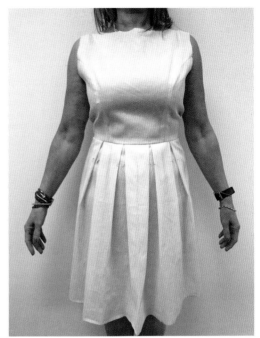

**Fig. 41    First toile of a dress with princess seams and pleated skirt.**

Fig. 40 shows the coat after the dart has been successfully lowered. It is now much better placed for this model.

## Princess Seams

Princess seams run from the shoulder or halfway down the armhole, down to or through the waist of a dress or top. If placed correctly, they are usually very flattering and can be a better fitting solution for many with bust-fitting problems, because they are much easier to alter than a garment with darts.

Fig. 41 shows a model in a dress with princess seams. At first sight the garment seems to fit reasonably well and the model said she felt quite comfortable. However, the drag lines (seen in Fig. 42 and described earlier in this chapter), from the bust down to the side waist and from the bust up towards the shoulder, immediately show that the fit is not as it should be. It may

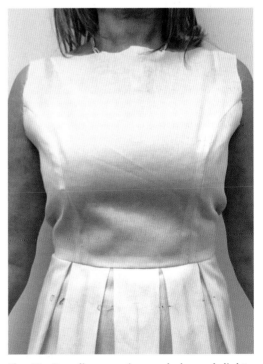

**Fig. 42    Drag lines, gaping armholes and slight gaping neck.**

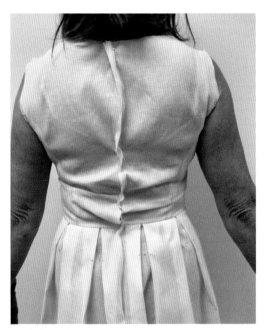

**Fig. 43   Dress seems too long at the back.**

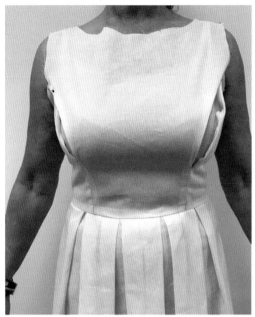

**Fig. 44   Releasing/opening up the bust seam to see how much needs to be added over the bust.**

also be that the princess seam is too curvy above the bust for this model and needs to be flattened out slightly, as well as being increased around the bust apex to make it fit better.

Looking up the bodice of the dress, it is also clear that the armhole is gaping slightly where the princess seam ends. The neck is gaping too. Turning the model around, we can see in Fig. 43 that the back of the dress is not lying correctly. The bunching of the fabric would suggest that the dress bodice is too long. But on reflection, it can be seen that the fabric is pulling from the side waist to the centre back seam, so it may be too tight somewhere instead.

The first thing to address is the fit at the bust, as this will have an impact on the whole dress. The princess seams on both sides of the dress bodice have been opened up (*see* Fig. 44) and the whole dress has 'relaxed' on the model. It is now clear that the fit at the bust is too small. The gaps that have opened up can be measured and tell us by how much the fit at the bust needs to be increased.

The next step is to address the gaping armhole. Fig. 45 shows that the princess seam has been opened up right through to the armhole and has been repinned to remove the excess fabric at the armhole edge. Realigning the seam in this way has also helped to remove some of the excess around the neck, because it has pulled the neck and shoulder out slightly. It has also removed some slight fullness above the bust.

**Note:** It may be that the measurements across the left and right seam openings differ from one another, with one larger than the other. As you will make alterations on a single pattern piece, take the larger of the two measurements as your alteration guide. If the differences are significant, then it is better to make the bodice suitable for the larger side and take in the smaller side slightly.

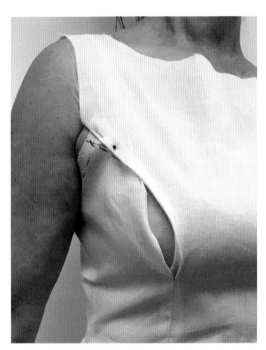

**Fig. 45** Pinning in the princess seam at the armhole to remove excess fabric.

**Fig. 46** Bust-fitting adjustments now made to the dress front – drag lines have disappeared.

These two key alterations – opening the seam over the bust and realigning the seam at the armhole – are undertaken first. It is important to only make one or two alterations at a time and then to refit the toile on the model. It may be that further alterations are still required, but it may also be that the alterations made have been sufficient to solve most of the fitting problems.

Figs 46 through 50 show the dress with the bust-fitting adjustments made. The bodice is now sitting well (Fig. 46) and the drag lines have disappeared. The excess fabric at the armhole has been removed and the neckline is less baggy. The side seams are hanging vertically (Fig. 47) and are not pulling either to the front or the back. If we look at the back of the dress in Fig. 48, we can see that the bunching has disappeared, and although it is close-fitting, as preferred by the model, the dress is sitting much better. Fig. 49 shows a slight length adjustment having been pinned at the waist and Fig. 50 shows the finished toile.

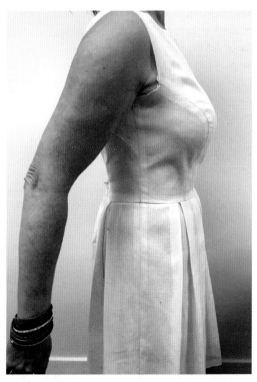

**Fig. 47** Side seams now hang vertically.

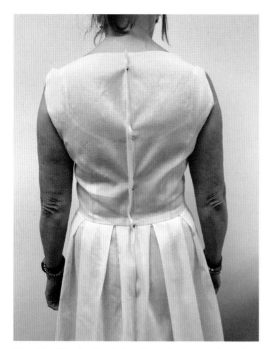

**Fig. 48   The back of the dress is more relaxed.**

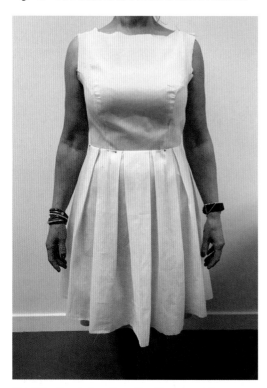

**Fig. 50   The toile after all adjustments have been made.**

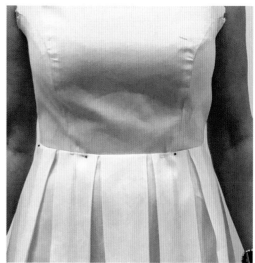

**Fig. 49   Slight length adjustment made at the waist.**

So, with this dress and for this model, addressing the fit at the bust has more or less solved all the other fitting issues that could be seen on the first toile. However, altering the fit at the bust may just be the first step in fitting your garment, and once that has been addressed, there may be other areas of fitting that need to be looked at. Neck and shoulders may need some adjustment after the fit at the bust has been corrected; back length may also need attention. If there are several adjustments to make, it is best to do them one at a time, because each fitting alteration will impact on the fit of the garment elsewhere. So be prepared for the fitting process to take some time.

Princess seams are not solely confined to the front of a garment. They are regularly used on the back of a garment too. Alterations to these seams are also often required. They are slightly easier to do, as they don't have to accommodate fitting a bust, and they are usually altered around the upper back and shoulders.

The princess seams on the back of the shirt shown in Figs 51 and 52 had to be altered more than those at the front. This model has slightly rounded shoulders and the seams had to be

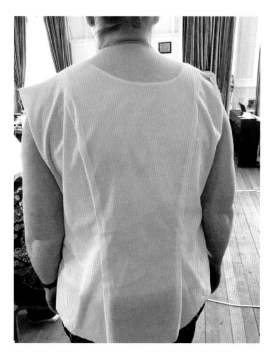

**Fig. 51  Princess seams on the back of a blouse.**

**Fig. 52  Neck darts added to remove slight fullness.**

realigned to take account of that. Once this was done, the shoulder seam was actually moved 1cm/½in towards the back, to give the illusion of a less-rounded shoulder for the wearer. You might also notice that a very small dart has been pinned into the neckline. This was to remove some fullness and gaping, and was a small enough alteration to transfer easily to the paper pattern. The overall result was very successful.

## Neck and Shoulders

Many of us need some adjustment at the neck and shoulders. For instance, many of us have one shoulder higher than the other. Sometimes a simple lift at the lowest shoulder will work with no adjustment needed for the other shoulder, and this can be done on the final garment. However, it may be that the shoulder is too wide or gaping and is affecting the armhole. Or perhaps the back shoulder needs better fitting.

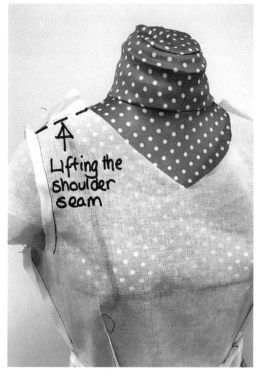

**Fig. 53  Realigning the shoulder seam.**

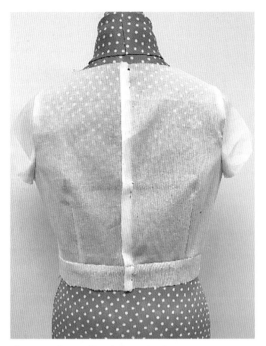

**Fig. 54  First toile of dress bodice.**

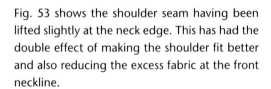

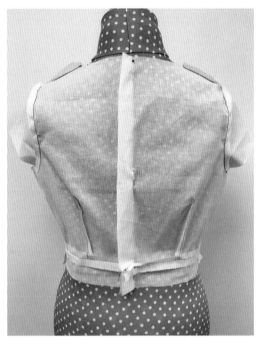

**Fig. 55  Back seam with excess fabric pinned out and darts lengthened slightly.**

Fig. 53 shows the shoulder seam having been lifted slightly at the neck edge. This has had the double effect of making the shoulder fit better and also reducing the excess fabric at the front neckline.

## Back and Shoulders

The back of the garment needs to fit properly, too. If it is too wide, it will be baggy across the back and at the centre seam or zip. If it is too tight, it will pull and restrict movement. If it is too long, then the garment will bunch around the middle; too short and the hips will not be sitting at the right level.

In Fig. 54 the dress bodice is quite large across the back and there is a clear excess of fabric above the darts. In Fig. 55 the toile has been turned inside out, the centre back seam of the dress taken in and the darts lengthened very slightly to remove the excess fabric.

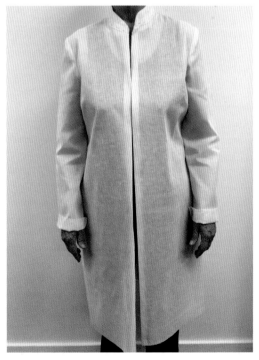

**Fig. 56  Toile of a coat with shoulders too wide and sleeves too long.**

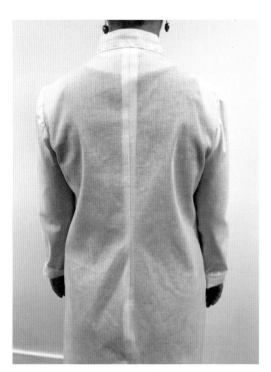

**Fig. 57** There also seems to be too much fabric in the back of this coat.

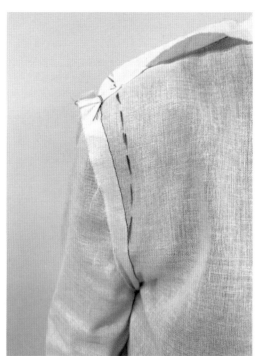

**Fig. 58** Marking where the shoulder seam needs to be.

Let's now go back to the coat we looked at when we discussed alterations to the placement of bust darts (Figs 56 and 57). We can immediately see that the shoulders are too wide and the sleeve is hanging off the shoulder. This is causing the back of the coat to hang badly and look as if it is much too big. It is also making the model look as if she has very sloping shoulders. It is also apparent that the sleeves are too long. They've been turned up to account for the sleeve hem, but might still need to be shortened slightly.

Fig. 58 shows the new shoulder seam line placement. This has been drawn onto the toile with a marker pen and has been placed closer to the shoulder tip and at the wearer's preferred position. Fig. 59 shows the toile with a sleeve removed ready to realign the shoulder seam. You might notice that as soon as the sleeve is removed and the shoulder relaxes, the back of the coat doesn't pull so much. Once

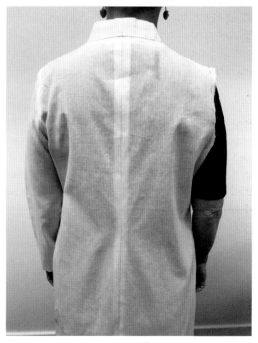

**Fig. 59** When the sleeve is removed, the back of the coat doesn't pull so much.

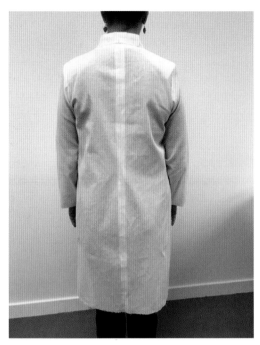 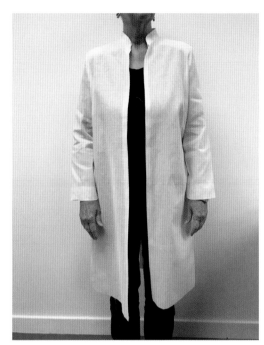

**Fig. 60   The toile after all alterations have been made.**

the shoulder seam is lifted, this should help the back of the coat sit much better.

These adjustments will all be transferred to the paper pattern and the toile remade to ensure that the alterations are correct.

Fig. 60 shows the finished toile after all alterations – including the adjustments to the bust dart position – have been made. The shoulder seams have both been shortened and realigned, and the sleeves reinserted. A light shoulder pad has been tacked into the coat to help it sit better, and the sleeves have been shortened at the hem. The back is hanging much better now that the shoulders have been adjusted and the coat is now a much better fit all round. In this case, the alterations made to the position of the bust dart were not enough in themselves to improve the fit of this garment.

## Waist and Tummy

This is an area that logically should be easier to adjust. It either needs to be taken in, or to be let out. However, it may be that a round tummy is causing the garment to strain and therefore the front hem of the garment is sitting high, or perhaps uneven hip height is causing a problem. Perhaps due to a fuller tummy, the front waistband of trousers or a skirt sits slightly under the tummy and lower than the back waistband, making the garment sit and hang unevenly.

## Hips

Hips don't normally cause many problems. The fit on them is either slightly large or a bit tight, and the remedy is to let them out or take them in. Depending on the style of garment and the wearer's preference, the fit at the hip can be altered relatively simply. Make sure you don't fit hips too closely unless the pattern design demands it. Fitting too tightly across the hips can make the fabric pull across the lower tummy and cause strain on the skirt, dress or trousers.

It looks much better if some ease across the hips is allowed, even in a stretch garment. The only time you want a really close fit is for dance wear, gym wear or swimwear.

## Body Length

If your garment is too long or short in the body, this will cause a couple of very obvious problems. First, if it is too long, the body will bunch up around the waist. This may not be so obvious in a garment with princess seams if the dress/top has a bit of ease in it. However, for a more fitted garment this will need to be adjusted. If the garment is too short in the body, the hip will be too high, or the garment will feel as if it is rising and you will be tempted to tug it down into place when wearing it.

## Finished Length

The finished overall length of your garment is very important. The design will dictate length with some options, but you must be comfortable with the length, otherwise you will not wear the garment. The easiest thing to do is either to add to or cut off length from the hem of a garment, and this will work for a fairly straight style of skirt, dress or trousers. However, if the garment has shape – either wide/flared or narrow – then altering at the hem will ultimately affect the overall style of the garment. For instance, if you are making a pair of bootleg trousers and you need to alter the length, adding length at the hem could make them into flared trousers. Conversely, taking length off at the hem could make them into straight-legged trousers. It is the same with skirts and dresses. A narrow skirt lengthened at the hem could become too narrow to walk in, and if shortened at the hem will lose its tulip shape. So choose carefully where to alter the length of your garment and use the lengthen/shorten lines if you are making an adjustment of more than a couple of centimetres/three-quarters of an inch.

Finished sleeve length usually depends on the wearer's choice. Sleeves can be shortened at the hem, or they can be shortened using the lengthen/shorten lines. If the sleeves need only a minor adjustment, then taking a little off the hem is perfectly acceptable. However, it is much more sensible to use the lengthen/shorten lines if the sleeves are very much too long. If the sleeves are too short, then the only way to lengthen them is to use the lengthen/shorten lines.

## Trousers

Trousers give us a whole lot of new fitting conundrums that are a little more tricky to understand. We all know what a great pair of trousers looks and feels like, but making a pair that looks and feels great can be a challenge. The problems usually occur because there is not enough crotch depth (known as the rise), and sometimes not enough length from front to back. Measuring the rise and the depth can be a little sensitive, and sometimes a solution is to take a pair of trousers that you have bought and feel good in and compare them to your new paper pattern.

If the rise is too short, then the trousers will cut into your buttocks; too long and there will be excess fabric in the seat. The depth of the trousers front to back can often be remedied by adjusting the rise. When increasing or decreasing the rise at the back of the trousers, it is important to remember to increase/decrease the side seam by the same amount to ensure a proper fit.

Once the rise has been adjusted and the fit is good, then waist and hip adjustments can be made, and finally leg width and length adjustments can also be made if needed.

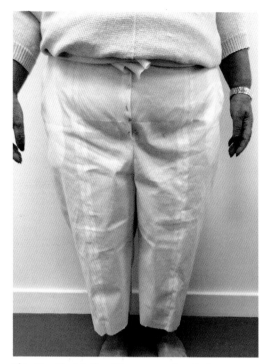

**Fig. 61   First toile of trousers – front view.**

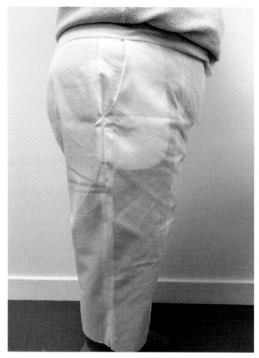

**Fig. 62   First toile of trousers – side view.**

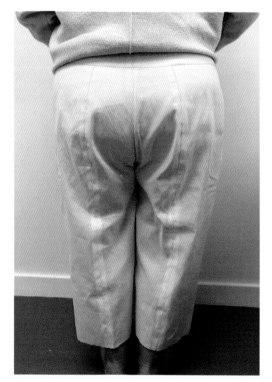

**Fig. 63   First toile of trousers – back view.**

In Figs 61, 62 and 63, you can see a first toile of a pair of cut-off trousers. On first inspection of the front fit of the trousers, they seem OK. The calico has become creased whilst putting the trousers on, and this is slightly distracting. The trousers fit around the waist and appear to fit on the hips, although the front crotch is hanging slightly low. From the side view (Fig. 62), we can see that the side seam is hanging vertically and there is no pull, so the trousers are not too tight anywhere. However, when we look at the back of the trousers (Fig. 63), we can see definite fitting issues that will need to be addressed.

The first thing to notice is the drag lines from the centre of the buttocks to the top of the inside thigh. This means that some part of the trousers is too tight. Because we haven't seen any other indications that the trousers are too tight, this probably means that the crotch rise/curve is not long enough, so the crotch seam is pulling into the buttocks. The solution is to

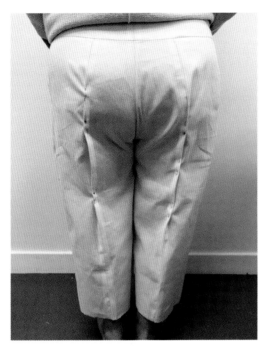

**Fig. 64  Back leg seams pinned in to remove excess fabric.**

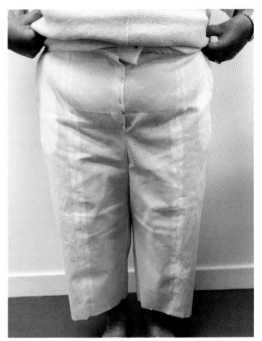

**Fig. 65  Trouser front after back seam pinned in.**

increase or deepen the curve (that is, make it more curvy). This will lengthen the curve and stop it pulling into the buttocks. We can also see the folds of fabric running alongside the drag lines from the centre back leg seam, again towards the upper inner thigh. Finally, further down the leg, nearer to the knee, there seems to be a lot of fabric.

The first adjustment is to pin out the excess fabric down the back of the leg, as seen in Fig. 64. The difference in the fit of the leg can be seen immediately, both on the back and on the front of the trousers. No adjustment has been made on the front seams of the trousers because this would affect the fit around the tummy, making the trousers pull in around the lower tummy and accentuating it. The trousers already look much better with the back seams pinned in, but now it can be seen (Fig. 65) that the waistband is folding over slightly in the centre of the model's tummy. This means that the front length is a little too long and needs

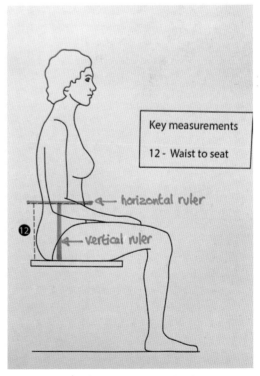

**Fig. 66  How to measure crotch rise.**

to be reduced. Once the length is reduced, this will probably also eliminate the impression that the front crotch is too low.

The second fitting adjustment is to the crotch rise/depth. This alteration is more tricky, because these are not such easy measurements to take. One way to measure the crotch rise is to sit the model on a table or flat surface and to measure from the table up to their side waist (*see* the measurement diagrams described in Chapter 2).

If you use two solid rulers, this will give a fairly accurate measurement (*see* Fig. 66). Use one ruler vertically alongside the model and another horizontally across the top of the first ruler, at waist level, making a 'T' shape with the rulers. Measure the height up from the table to the waist.

Measuring crotch length (front to back) is much more sensitive and not all models are comfortable with having this measurement taken. The crotch length can be measured with a tape measure from centre front waist, between the legs and up to centre back waist. The front crotch length measurement then needs to be separated from the back crotch length measurement. In this case, a judgement has been made that approximately 2cm or ¾in needs to be taken out of the crotch curve on the back of the trousers.

## TIP: MEASURING THE CROTCH LENGTH AND RISE

If you and your model find measuring the crotch length is too close and personal, take a close-fitting pair of trousers belonging to the model and measure the crotch curves on the trousers. These measurements will not be totally accurate, but should give a good guide.

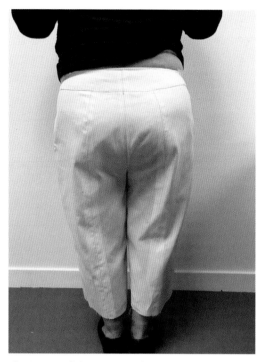

**Fig. 67 Back leg seams taken in and crotch curve increased.**

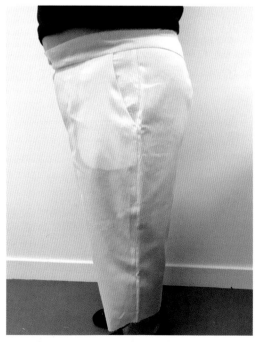

**Fig. 68 Front waistband has been dropped slightly for better fit under the tummy.**

When increasing the crotch length, to make the curve more rounded or deeper, it is important to understand that you are taking away some of the width of the trousers because you have actually cut away up to 1cm/½in from the crotch seam. To compensate for this, the same amount that is taken from the crotch length should be added to the side seam, at the hip area, to ensure a proper fit. In this case, because the trousers were actually a little too big, the crotch length has been increased/adjusted in isolation, without needing to add any width to the side seams.

Fig. 67 shows the altered toile with the centre back leg seams taken in and the crotch curve increased. The centre front waist has also been

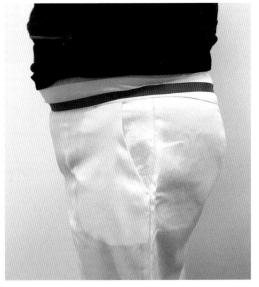

**Fig. 69   Back waistband is too low and needs to be lifted.**

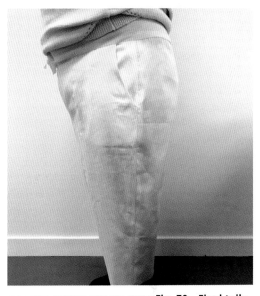

TOP RIGHT, BOTTOM LEFT AND RIGHT: **Fig. 70   Final toile of trousers with crotch curve increased, front waistband dropped and back waistband raised.**

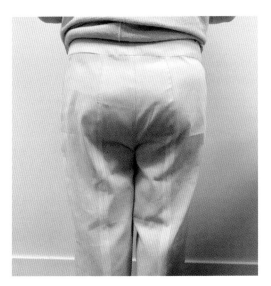

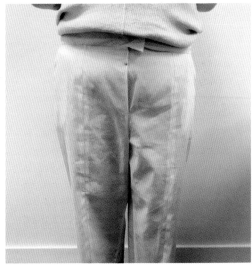

## TIP: TROUSER FITTING

Don't overfit your trousers. If you do, you run the risk of emphasizing a round tummy, or making the crotch fitting too tight, or causing the fabric to pull across the front crotch in an unattractive way. Fitting trousers sometimes has to be a compromise.

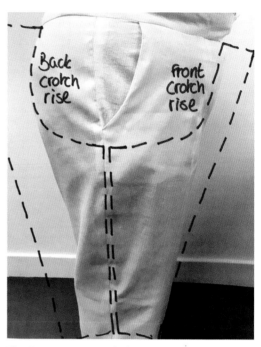

**Fig. 71   How a rounded crotch curve looks on a pattern piece.**

dropped slightly. A small amount has been taken off the length at the centre front and graduated up to the side waist, which has not been altered (Fig. 68). The fit is clearly much better. However, when the model turns sideways (Fig. 69), we can see that the waistband is dipping at the back. This model needs a slight adjustment to drop the waist at the front of the trousers, but the back waist needs lifting as well. In other words, the crotch length on the back of the trousers needs to be increased again to lift the waistband up to where it should more naturally rest. A piece of coloured tape has been placed around the model's tummy to show how much the centre back seam needs to be lifted.

Fig. 70 shows the waist adjustment at the back and the overall much improved fit of the trousers front and back.

**Note:** These trousers have a centre front and centre back seam down the legs. Most trouser patterns don't have this. However, all trouser patterns can have fullness taken out of the legs in the same way as has been done in this example. The centre back or front of the trouser leg can be pinned in to remove excess fullness from the leg, and this alteration is easily transferred to the paper pattern. Removing fullness from the centre of the trouser leg in this way does not affect the style of the trousers at all.

So far we have discussed how to increase the crotch curve to fit rounder, fuller buttocks. In Fig. 71 pattern pieces have been drawn around the model to show how the crotch curve may need to be increased for a better fit. The opposite can be done to fit flatter buttocks, as seen in Fig. 72. In this case, the crotch curve might need to be reduced or flattened out. If this is done, then the side seams may also need to be reduced/taken in at the hip area by the same amount in order to ensure a comfy and neat fit.

Fitting trousers is definitely more tricky than fitting most other garments, and there is often a temptation to continue to make adjustments to a pair of trousers to get the fit better and better. However, it is sensible not to 'overfit' trousers and to recognize that there will be some fitting compromises when working with trousers. It is also very important to think of comfort when fitting trousers. If trousers are fitted very tightly across the hips, then there will be some pull in the fabric. If the crotch fitting needs to be more

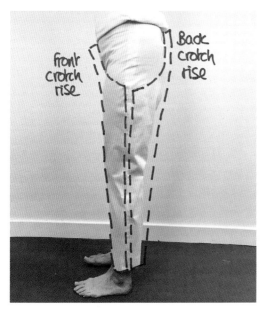

**Fig. 72  How a flatter crotch curve looks on a pattern piece.**

relaxed, then there will be some extra fabric in the trousers across the hip/thigh area. We are our own worst critics – so don't be too critical of your efforts!

## Marking Adjustments on the Toile

This is the really interesting part of fitting! You will need a tape measure, scissors, a seam ripper, pins and a marker pen. Stand back and look at the garment on the wearer. As you look, you will begin to see what's not quite right. Go to the first and most obvious fitting problem. It may be that you will have to open a seam or part of a seam to allow the garment to lie better, so unpick it whilst it is still on the wearer or the dressform. This will let you know if fabric needs to be added to that area of the garment or if the seam needs to be taken in or realigned. If opening the seam allows the garment to lie better, you can either repin the seam, pin

a piece of fabric into the space that has been created, marking carefully on the toile what you have done, or, if the alteration is relatively small, just use pins if you can and write on the toile exactly what alteration needs to be made.

The jacket in Fig. 73 is being fitted on a dress-form. The draglines from the bust to the side hip can be seen clearly. However, when pinning the jacket at the front, the bust seems to fit well. Therefore, the jacket must be too tight across the upper hip, and that is what is causing the draglines. The side seam has then been opened slightly. This has allowed the jacket to 'relax', and we can see quite clearly that a small altera-tion needs to be made from the waist to the upper hip. The width of the opening across from seam line to seam line can be measured, as can the length of the opening in the seam from top to bottom, and the length from the underarm to where the seam has been opened (Fig. 74). These measurements can then be transferred to the pattern. It's a good idea to write on the toile with a marker pen exactly what alteration is required and where it needs

**Fig. 73  Drag lines on a jacket being fitted on a dressform.**

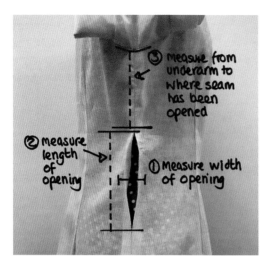

**Fig. 74   How to measure the alterations for transfer to the paper pattern.**

to begin and end. Fewer mistakes are made that way, and it also saves time. Turn the toile inside out – this will make it much easier to mark and pin. Remember to mark adjustments that only need to be made on one side of the body, such as a high shoulder or hip, on the right side of the toile to ensure that the alterations are made in the correct place.

Figs. 75, 76 and 77 show the toile turned

inside out. We can now see folds of fabric running down the back of the jacket from the shoulders to the waist area (Fig. 75). This means there is too much fabric, or the jacket is too wide across the shoulder and upper back area. In Fig. 76 the centre back seam has been pinned in slightly and the darts have been increased. Both of these adjustments have now reduced the fullness across the upper back of the jacket. In Fig. 77 the jacket has been removed from the dressform, with the alterations marked clearly in red marker pen ready to be transferred to the pattern pieces.

Figs 78 and 79 show the bodice of a dress where the centre back seam has been repinned and the dart has been lengthened slightly. This is because, when fitting, it was found that the back of the dress was too wide. The centre back seam was taken in and pinned, and the dart was increased slightly in length. Both alterations were marked in red marker pen. Both of these alterations were made quite simply and effectively without upsetting the back of the dress, thus giving a much better fit.

Make as many adjustments as you sensibly can, marking them with pins and using

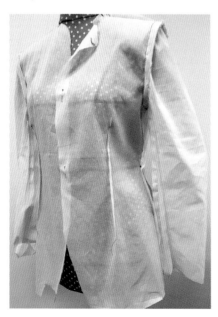

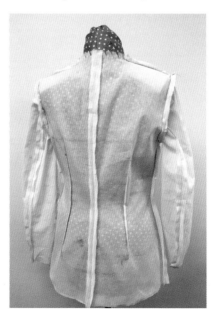

**Fig. 75
Jacket toile
turned inside
out and ready
for altering.**

a marker pen to draw in new seam lines, dart placements and other instructions as fitting requires. Try to make your marks as tidy and accurate as possible, because you will be using them to transfer the fitting adjustments to the paper pattern. It is important to remember,

however, to make only one or two adjustments at a time. They may be sufficient to make the garment fit really well, or they may be only a part of the fitting requirements, and will either alleviate any further fitting issues or will allow more accurate fitting to be continued.

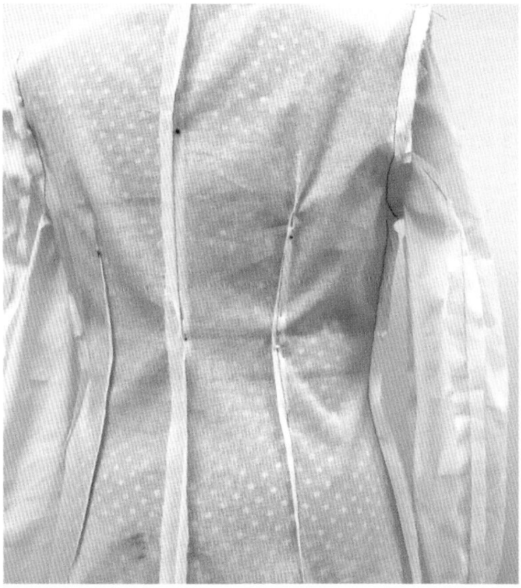

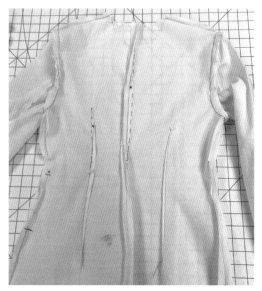

Fig. 76 Jacket toile with back seam pinned in and darts extended.

Fig. 77 ´ Ready to transfer alterations to the paper pattern.

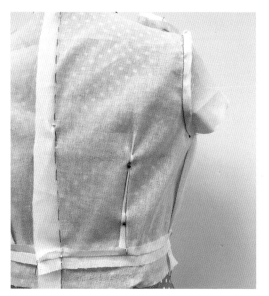

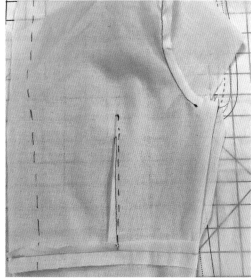

Fig. 78 Dress bodice with alterations pinned and marked with marker pen.

Fig. 79 Ready to transfer alterations to the paper pattern.

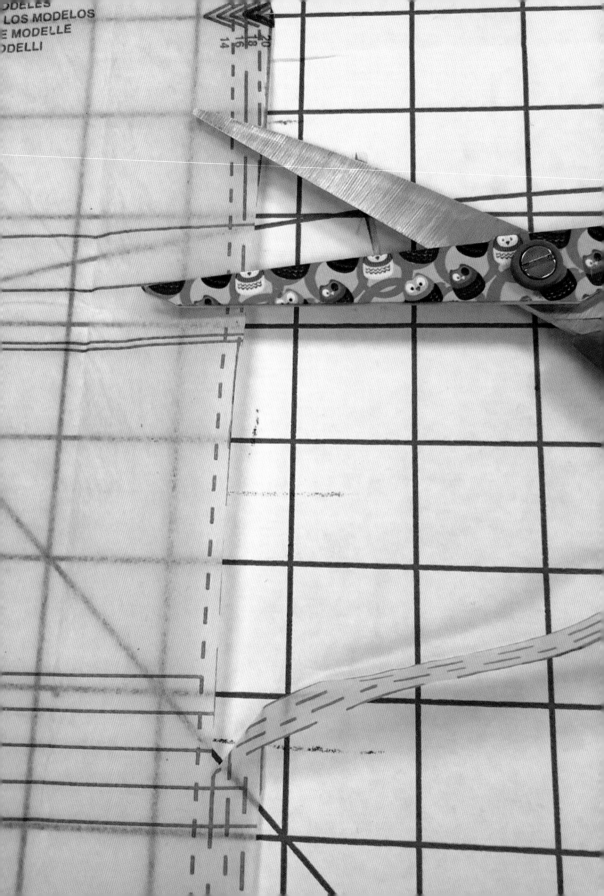

# ALTERING THE PAPER PATTERN

We are finally getting closer to having a pattern that works really well for us. It is a very satisfying feeling to know that all the hard work of making the toile and fitting the pattern is going to result in a garment that fits us so well that we'll want to make it again!

Before we get there, however, we have to transfer those fitting adjustments onto our paper pattern. For this, you need a French curve, plus a fine-tipped pen, a tape measure, pattern tracing paper and magic tape (sticky tape). All these tools will help you to make good alterations to your paper pattern.

## Transferring Fitting Adjustments to the Paper Pattern

The first thing to do is to lay your toile on your sewing table and check the markings you have made. Are they clear? Can you understand the adjustments you have made? Can you measure them well enough to transfer them to your paper pattern? If not, then take 10 minutes to put the toile back onto the wearer and go over your fitting changes again, using extra pins or marker pen to make sure that you know exactly what alterations you have to make to your paper pattern.

Take each alteration separately and make your changes to your pattern tissue slowly and

carefully. This will involve cutting and sticking and changing your pattern, so you don't want to make too many mistakes. Remember, mistakes can be rectified with more pattern tissue and sticky tape – but better not to make them at all, if possible.

Fig. 80 shows the back of a dress bodice where the centre back seam needs to be taken in and the dart lengthened slightly. The markings are clearly made in red marker pen and can be measured easily for transfer to the pattern piece.

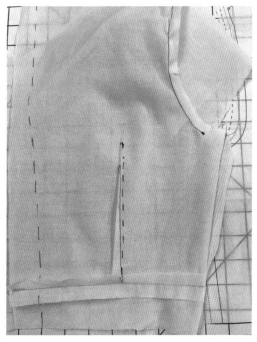

**Fig. 80   Dress bodice with alterations marked on it.**

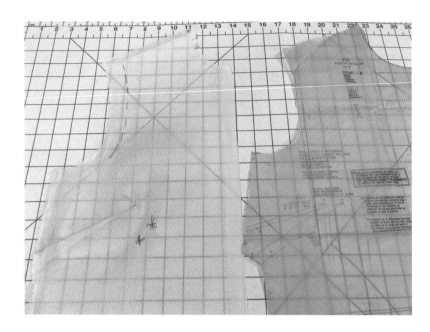

**Fig. 81** Coat piece and matching pattern piece, ready for marking fitting alterations.

Fig. 81 shows the front of a coat and the two black marks denote the new dart apex/point. There should only be one mark, but the apex/point was marked a second time to ensure that it was in the right place. If you make a change like this, then mark the alteration you actually want to make clearly on the toile before trans-

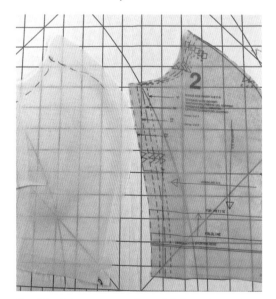

**Fig. 82** Princess seam dress fabric and pattern pieces ready for marking fitting alterations.

ferring the adjustment to the pattern tissue, in order that you make the correct or preferred change. In this case, the lower of the marks will be the one that is used. The higher mark will move the dart a little too much into the centre of the coat and may not look so good.

In Fig. 82 we can see the side front of the princess seam dress, shown earlier in the book. Here we can see that a new seam line has been drawn at the top of the side bodice. The new seam line has been marked only partially, because it graduates into the existing seam line.

Now we take our fine-tipped pen, tape measure and French curve. The French curve has a straight side and a graduated curved side ending in a rounded end. The trick with using a French curve is to find the part of the curve that will help us draw the best line/curve, and we often use several parts of the curve to make one smooth alteration.

In Fig. 83, you can see that a part of the French curve has been found that is very close to the alteration that we need to make on the princess seam side front (as shown in Fig. 82). You can just see the black marker pen underneath the curve, and a new red line has been

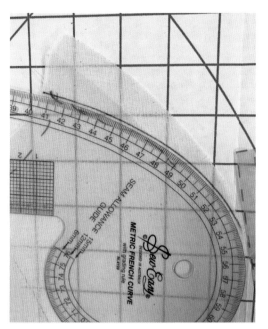

**Fig. 83   Using the French curve to measure the required alteration on the toile.**

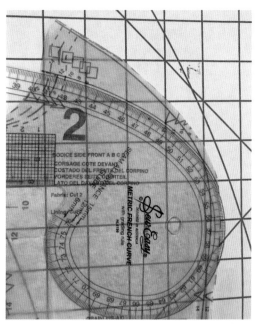

**Fig. 84   Transferring the alteration to the pattern piece.**

drawn on the toile that gives a smooth alteration and that follows the alteration that was pinned and marked on the toile. A trick with using the curve is to look at the numbers on the curve at either end of the alteration. In Fig. 83, the numbers you can see at the ends of the curve where it starts and finishes on the fabric, are 40.5cm on the left and 51cm on the right.

Moving to the paper pattern (Fig. 84), we must measure exactly where the new seam line is to be placed. To find the point on the armhole seam where the new seam line will begin, measure down from the cut edge of the armhole on the toile to the new seam line that is marked with a marker pen with your tape measure. Go to your paper pattern and measure down to the same point as on the toile. Then lay your ruler on the pattern starting at 40.5cm on the left-hand side. Move the ruler until it runs off the pattern at 54cm on the right-hand side (bust seam) of the pattern piece. If you do this, you will have copied exactly the curve made on your toile. Mark your paper tissue with the fine-

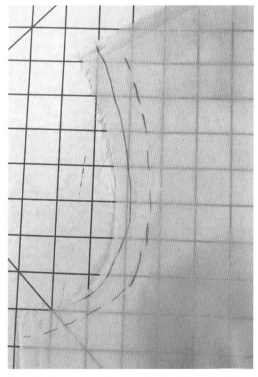

**Fig. 85   New seam line marked with dashed line and new cutting line marked in red.**

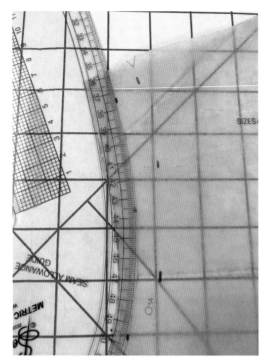

**Fig. 86 Transferring the armhole adjustments to the pattern piece.**

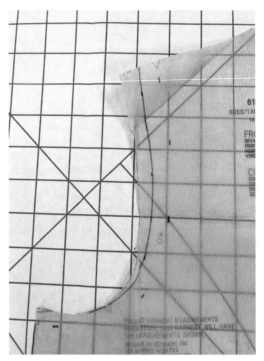

**Fig. 87 Fitting adjustments drawn onto the pattern piece.**

tipped pen, remembering that this is your new seam line, so you must add a seam allowance to that alteration. To do this, you should mark 1.5cm/5/8in up and out from the line you have just drawn, and draw a second curve that will graduate more quickly into the original cutting line on the pattern piece. Fig. 85 shows how to add a seam allowance, where the new armhole seam line has been marked on the toile in a black dashed line and the new pattern cutting line, a solid line, has been marked in red. Fig. 86 shows the new seam line on the paper pattern marked in dots (quite far apart), and the new pattern cutting line along the length of the French curve. Fig. 87 shows where the paper pattern will be cut along the solid red line to make the final alteration to the armhole.

If this all seems hugely complicated, take it one step at a time. First, measure the new seam line. Then add a seam allowance. Draw the seam line in with a dotted line and the seam allowance line with a solid line. The solid line becomes the new cutting line where you need to remove the excess pattern tissue.

The second way of doing this is to lay your pattern tissue piece over the toile piece – if you can! Then you can trace through from the toile to the pattern tissue. Be careful to make sure that your measurements are correct and your lines are drawn smoothly, if you make your pattern tissue alterations with this method.

# Making a Full Bust Adjustment

There are two types of full bust adjustment (FBA) that we can make. The first is on a princess seam and the second is around bust darts. The princess seam adjustment is actually much easier to fit and can give better results for the less-experienced sewer, so if you regularly have to make an FBA, consider using patterns with princess seams for a more flattering look and less stressful pattern adjustment.

## Full Bust Adjustments on a Princess Seam

If we refer back to the pictures of the princess seam dress used earlier in this book, we will remember that an FBA had to be made to the dress. The bust seams were opened up, as seen in Fig. 88, and the opening was measured to see how much needed to be added to the seam.

It was decided to increase the side front panel of the dress only and not the centre front panel. This is because the width of the front panel suited the wearer and the seams were lying just to the outside of the bust apex. If the front panel had been considered too narrow and the seams too far into the centre of the dress, then

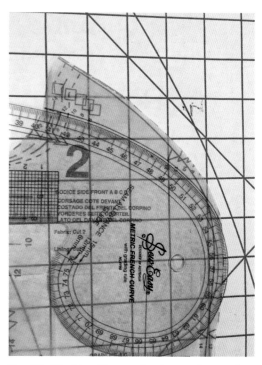

**Fig. 89  Marking the new bust seam line on the toile.**

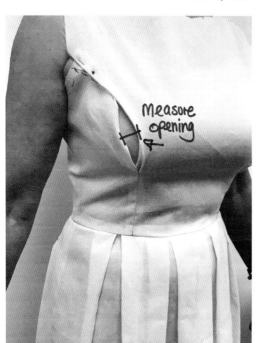

**Fig. 88  Measuring by how much to increase the bust area.**

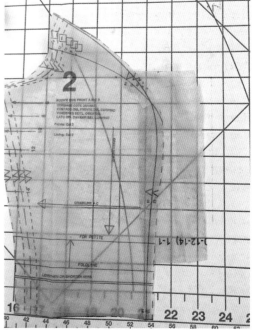

**Fig. 90  Adding tissue to the pattern piece to allow the extra curve to be drawn in.**

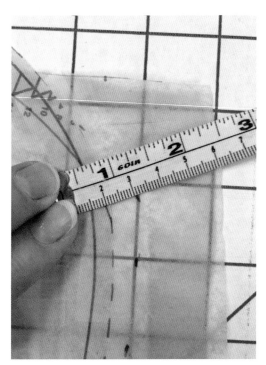

**Fig. 91   Adding extra allowance to the bust curve.**

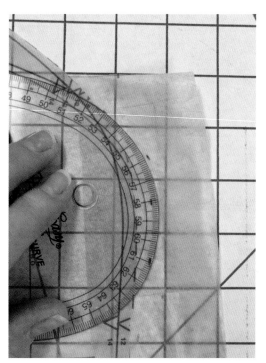

**Fig. 92   Using the French curve to draw in the bust adjustment.**

the measurement taken from the opening in the seam would have been divided in two, with half added to each of the side front panel seam and the centre panel seam of the dress front.

The first mark to make on the paper pattern is the new seam line, as described earlier in this chapter (*see* Fig. 89). Now we must add to the pattern piece. We take a piece of pattern tissue (either kept from cutting out the pattern or purchased pattern tissue) and attach it with tape to the area of the pattern that needs to be increased, as shown in Fig. 90. The measurement that we took when the dress was on the model is now transferred to the extra tissue around the bust point of the paper pattern, that is, the sharpest and curviest part of the pattern, as seen in Fig. 91. Then we graduate the measurement back to the seam allowance above and below that point.

Now we take the French curve and use it to 'join the dots'. Try and make a smooth transi-

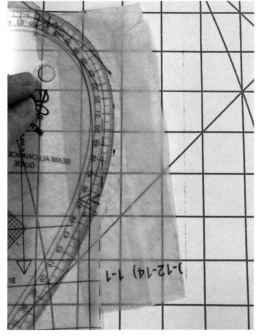

**Fig. 93   Matching the curve of the adjustment to the French curve.**

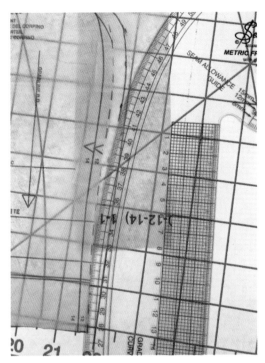

**Fig. 94  Turning the French curve over.**

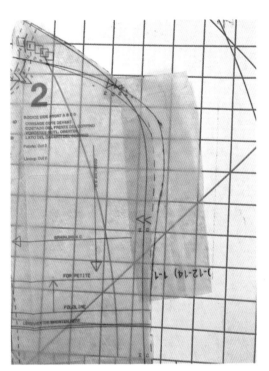

**Fig. 95  Alteration made and excess pattern tissue ready to be cut away.**

tion from the new seam line into the bust curve using one part of the French curve (*see* Fig. 92). Then use another bit of the French curve, as demonstrated in Fig. 93, to achieve a smooth bust curve. Finally, flip the French curve over, as shown in Fig. 94, making the curve concave, to finish drawing the alteration and to gradu-ate it smoothly from the new bust curve into the existing seam allowance at the waist. You should end up with an alteration looking like the one shown in Fig. 95, and you are now ready to cut off the excess tissue. Remember to redraw your notch on the side front panel.

Although we have decided not to add anything to the seam allowance at the centre front panel, we still have an alteration to make to that panel. The reason for this is that we have actually *increased* the length of the curve on the side front panel. Therefore, we need to add a small amount of length to the centre front panel as well, otherwise it will be too short when we sew the pieces together.

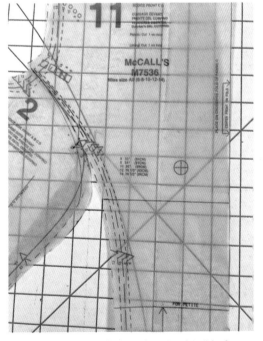

**Fig. 96  Matching the notches on the side front panel and the front panel of the dress.**

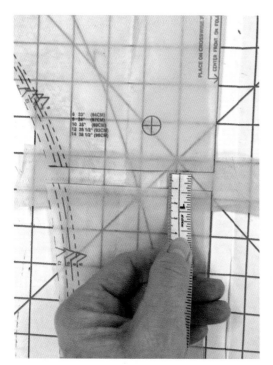

**Fig. 97 Lengthening the front panel of the dress.**

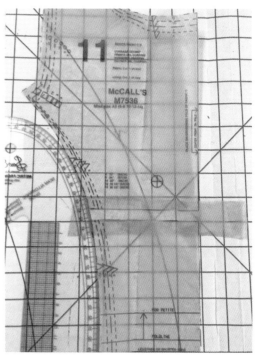

**Fig. 98 How to true your cutting lines after making pattern alterations.**

Take your pattern pieces and lay them together, as shown in Fig. 96. Match the notches at the top of the bust curve and then locate the bust apex area on the side panel. Draw a horizontal line on the centre front panel at this point. Make sure that the line you draw is square to the grainline or foldline of the pattern piece. Then cut the centre front panel in two across your drawn in line. The next step is to add a piece of pattern tissue and tape it to the top part of the front panel. Line up the bottom half of the pattern piece and carefully measure the distance between the two pieces. In this case 1cm/½in has been added to the length of the centre front panel (see Fig. 97). When you have your pieces lined up and measured, carefully tape the bottom half of the pattern piece to the inserted pattern tissue. Finally, use your French curve to 'true' your cutting lines, which is to smooth them out, as demonstrated in Fig. 98, and trim off the excess tissue on either side. Your pattern is now ready to use.

## Full Bust Adjustment on a Darted Bodice/Dress

If you are making a dress or top with a darted bodice and you have to increase the bust size or make a full bust adjustment, the process is slightly different, but the principle is the same. Extra room must be made to accommodate the bust.

The first step is to refer back to the personal body measurements. Take the high bust measurement and the full bust measurement and subtract one from the other. If, for example, the high bust is 106cm/42in and the full bust 116cm/46in, the difference is 10cm/4in. This is the amount that needs to be added to the overall bust measurement. Divide the amount by two, and that will give you the total increase to be made at the bust on the front pattern piece.

**Calculating Your Increase:** if you need to increase the bust by 5cm/2in, then divide that total increase by two to get 2.5cm/1in. This is the amount by which you will increase your single pattern piece. The reason for this is that when you cut the fabric pieces again, you will be cutting either two separate pieces, or one on the fold, and the amount you have added will be doubled up when the fabric pieces are cut and ready to sew.

Figs 99, 100 and 101 show the next steps described below:

1. Mark a line about two-thirds of the way down the armhole to the bust point/apex.
2. Draw a line from the bust point/apex down to the hemline of the garment, ensuring it is straight and parallel to the grainline.
3. Mark a line directly through the middle of the side dart, if there is one, to the dart point. In this example there is no side dart, only a waist dart. So draw the third line directly across to the bust point, stopping where a dart would finish. Use your judgement here.
4. Cut all these lines, making sure not to cut through the armhole but just up to the armhole, so that the pattern can 'hinge' to one side. Also make sure you only cut through the dart to the dart point and not right through to the bust point/apex. Our pattern tissue is now effectively in three pieces, held together, almost precariously, at the armhole and the dart point.
5. Slide the pattern pieces carefully apart until the space between the bust point/apex and the pattern tissue nearest the dart point is

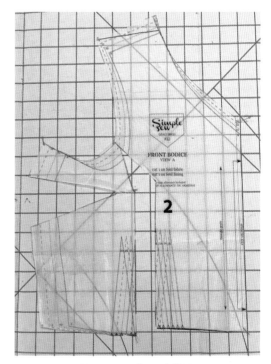

**Fig. 99  Preparing to make a full bust adjustment.**

the same as the measurement calculated for increasing the bust (that is, half the total increase required). Then fix the pattern so that it doesn't move; use pins in your cutting board or pattern weights. You will notice that the bust dart will get wider as the whole side of the pattern moves to the left.
6. Now straighten up the side piece of the pattern tissue so that it is lying parallel to the long vertical cut line. At this point you will have to make some small folds in the pattern tissue at the armhole and at the bust dart point to help the pattern tissue once again lie flat. When all the pattern pieces are realigned, slide pattern tissue paper underneath and fill in the spaces that have been created by cutting the tissue open and moving it. Fix the pattern tissue in the spaces with tape to make your final adjusted pattern piece.

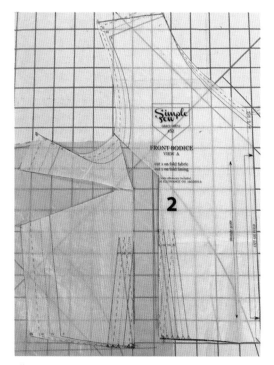

Fig. 100   Using pattern tissue to fill in the spaces.

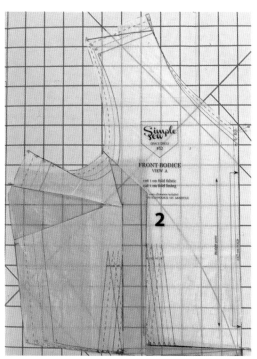

Fig. 101   Pattern altered and ready to use.

You will notice that a dart has been created at the side seam where there was no dart before. This often happens with a larger bust adjustment and is almost unavoidable if a good fit is the aim. True out the ends of the dart and check it properly for fit and shape when making a second toile.

Finally, you will almost certainly have a difference in length between the left-hand side and the right-hand side of the pattern piece (see Fig. 101), and this will be seen at the hem of the garment. The right-hand side or centrefold side of the pattern piece should now be shorter than the left-hand side of the pattern piece. It is important to lengthen the right-hand side of the pattern piece to match the longer left-hand side, otherwise the garment will rise at the front hem and will not lie properly. The reason for the length difference is that a full bust adjustment actually needs more length in the pattern to cover the fuller bust.

Once alterations to the paper pattern have been completed, you will also need to ensure that the front and back side seams are the same length. You may need to true the front side seam of your pattern before you are finally ready to make your garment.

## Making a Small Bust Adjustment

Once again, there are two main adjustments that can be made for a small bust. One is to a princess seam dress or top and the other to a darted dress or top. Both processes are the same as for a full bust adjustment, but the opposite actions are taken: the princess seam is flattened out instead of being increased and the darted bodice is reduced instead of increased.

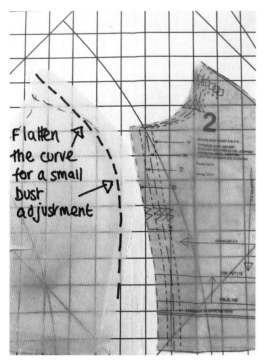

**Fig. 102   Flattening the bust curve on a princess seam.**

## Small Bust Adjustment on a Princess Seam

Making a small bust adjustment (SBA) on a princess seam dress or top follows the same process as described for an FBA, only this time you will *flatten out* the curve and effectively make it slightly shorter.

In Fig. 102 we can see how the curve is being reduced for the smaller bust. This will have the overall effect of reducing the length of the side panel of the dress or bodice. You will remember that making a full bust adjustment actually lengthened the side panel of the dress. As a result of flattening out the curve on the side panel, the centre front panel of the dress will almost certainly be longer. You should check which length fits the wearer best and either shorten the centre front panel by the appropriate amount or lengthen the side panel, if necessary.

## Small Bust Adjustment on a Darted Bodice/Dress

Making a small bust adjustment in a dress or top with bust darts again follows the same process as for making a full bust adjustment. In a full bust adjustment, the pattern piece is made bigger or expanded. A small bust adjustment requires us to compress the pattern piece, to make it smaller around the bust area.

In Fig. 103 we can see that the pattern piece has been cut exactly the same way as it was for the full bust adjustment. A red line has been drawn from about two-thirds of the way down the armhole to the bust point/apex. A second line has been drawn from the bust apex straight down through the waist dart, and a third line has been cut approximately where a side seam dart would be placed. These lines have been cut open, making sure not to cut through the armhole but just up to the armhole, so that the pattern can 'hinge' to one side at the armhole.

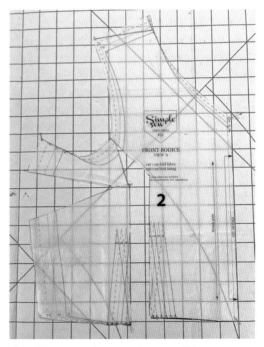

**Fig. 103   Preparing to make a small bust adjustment.**

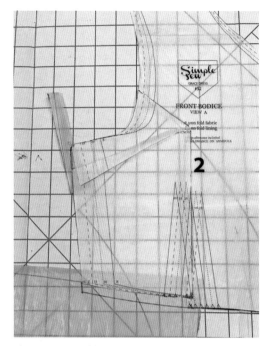

**Fig. 104   Small bust adjustment made.**

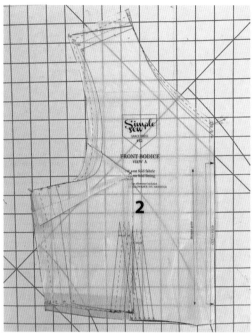

**Fig. 105   Pattern altered and ready to use.**

The pattern has also only been cut through the dart area to the dart point and not right through to the bust point/apex.

As before, the pattern tissue is effectively divided into three pieces, held together at the armhole and the dart point. This time, instead of the pattern piece being opened out, it has been 'squashed together' and the cut lines have been overlapped. Once again, if the total reduction to the bust measurement needs to be, for example, 2.5cm/1in, that amount must be halved to 1.75cm/½in, and this is the measurement for the total overlap. That is, the cut edges of the pattern should overlap each other by 0.8cm/¼in. Use pattern tissue and tape to fix the adjusted pattern piece and to realign the hemline at the side front. As a result of reducing the bust measurement in this way, the side of the pattern piece has moved up slightly, so the hemline needs to be returned to its original length, or to the length determined through fitting.

The bust dart will also change in a small bust adjustment. In this example, the dart comes from the waist up. Find the original size of dart used to make the toile and redraw the dart legs following those size guides. Keep in mind that the dart will have reduced in size or width at its widest end because of the bust alteration to pattern piece.

A side bust dart must be moved in the same way. When you move the bottom left-hand side of the pattern piece to overlap it with the right side, the bust dart will naturally move too and will become smaller. Once the alteration is firmly taped in place, it will be necessary to redraw the side bust dart, following existing dart lines and to true out the side seam. In this example, there is no side dart, so the side seam simply needs to be straightened out or 'trued'.

## Moving Darts

Sometimes, the bust darts on patterns are just

not in the right place for us. Very often we will make do with the dart placement, but if we can learn how to move the dart, then the final garment will look so much better. The most common bust dart movement concerns the dart that comes from the side seam across and up to the bust. But we can move shoulder darts and waist darts in exactly the same way.

## Moving a Dart Up or Down

Figs 106, 107 and 108 demonstrate how to move a dart. The first thing to do is to draw a rectangular box around the dart. Keep it neat and as close to the dart as you can. Mark on the paper pattern where the dart apex needs to be moved to. This can be seen in Fig. 107 as a small horizontal line on the right-hand side of the box. This mark has been measured straight down from the existing dart apex and according to what was marked on the toile.

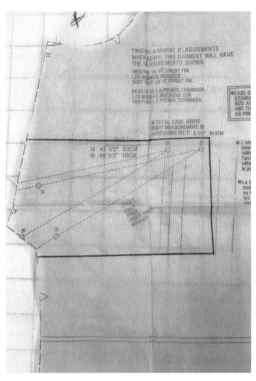

Fig. 106   **Marking out the dart for moving.**

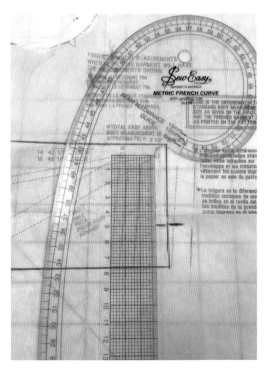

Fig. 107   **Marking the new dart apex.**

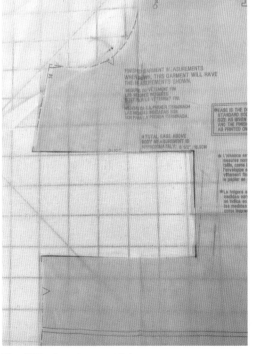

Fig. 108   **Dart 'rectangle' cut out.**

Cut out the box (*see* Fig. 108) and move it down the pattern until the pattern dart apex is aligned with the new dart apex that you have measured and marked. Make sure that your box is square and parallel to the grain line so that you know that the dart apex has not moved left or right and that it hasn't twisted. Secure the box with tape, making sure that it is properly square to the pattern (*see* Fig. 109). You will now have a big hole in your pattern piece above your dart, so take some pattern tissue and attach it to the underneath side of your pattern to fill in the space you have made (*see* Fig. 110). Finally, with your French curve true out the side seam of the pattern with the most suitable part of the curve that you can find, as demonstrated in Fig. 111.

Fig. 112 shows how your pattern should look after successfully moving the dart and trimming off the excess pattern tissue.

This process can also be used to move a dart upwards. There may not be so much leeway for

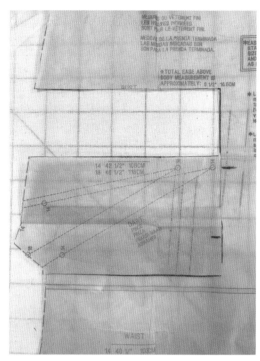

**Fig. 109   Dart dropped and taped into new position.**

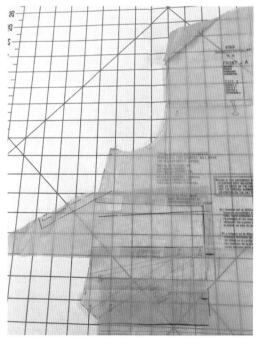

**Fig. 110   Spare pattern tissue used to fill in the gap.**

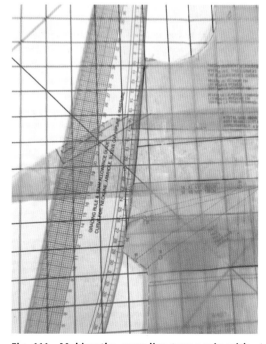

**Fig. 111   Making the seam line true again with the French curve.**

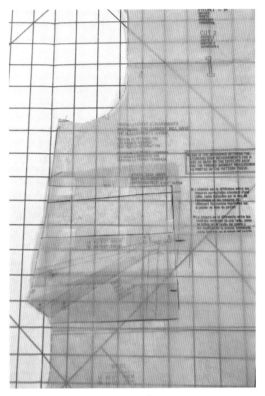

**Fig. 112    Pattern piece ready to use.**

moving a dart up, as it could end up quite close to the armhole seam. However, most darts only need to be moved by a small amount, so moving the dart upwards shouldn't create any problems.

You can also raise a dart by lifting the shoulders of the garment until the dart is in the right place, and then opening out or increasing the armhole at the underarm. This has the same result. The key alterations in this case are to the underarm part of the armhole and to the body length of the garment. The reasons for this are that, by lifting the shoulders, you will have decreased the size of the armhole, so it will need to be opened up/increased at the underarm. The reason for lengthening the body of the garment is because, again, by lifting the shoulders, you will have raised the waist and hips so that they are now too high. You should use the lengthen and shorten lines to add the

amount you have taken off at the shoulders to the overall body length.

## Moving a Dart Sideways

Moving a dart sideways is done in exactly the same way as moving a dart up or down. Mark on the toile where the preferred placement of either end of the dart should be. Go to your pattern tissue and draw a box around the dart on the pattern piece. Cut out the box and move it to the right or left by the amount decided when fitting the toile. Finally, fill in the space created by cutting out the box with some spare pattern tissue and tape carefully.

Be careful not to move the dart too much, otherwise it might unbalance the look of the garment. Also, it's a good idea to check the pattern envelope and look at the drawings/ photos of the garment and see where the dart is placed. This will guide you as to where the design of the garment suggests the dart should be.

## Lengthening/Shortening Darts

We tend to accept the darts that we find on a pattern as fixed and we don't always realize we can move them, as described above, or lengthen and shorten them if that suits our fitting requirements. For instance, it may be that double-ended darts that run from under the bust down towards the hips would be better shortened at the top of the dart for a fuller-busted figure, or over the tummy if the darts are causing the skirt of a dress to be a bit tight.

In the same way, we can lengthen darts a little to take out some fullness in a garment, if that suits the fit and the look of the garment. In Fig. 113, we can see the back of a dress bodice being fitted on a dressform, and probably the first thing we see is that the bodice is too big.

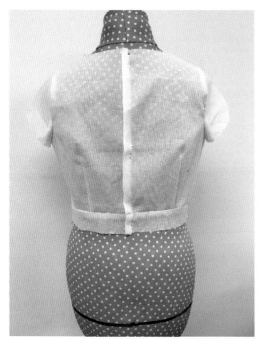

**Fig. 113 Dress bodice before any alterations are made.**

There is a lot of extra fabric above the darts and across the upper back. Fig. 114 shows the toile turned inside out on the dressform and the back seam taken in. (Remember, it's much easier to pin alterations into the toile if it is inside out.) Fig. 115 shows that the darts have also been lengthened slightly. They have been pinned in a little without being made too long, and both alterations have made enough of a difference to the fit of the bodice.

Once the alterations have been pinned and marked onto the toile, it is taken off the dress-form and laid beside the pattern piece. Then the fitting alterations are carefully copied onto the pattern tissue. The new dart apex is measured, on the toile, from the original apex (dart finishing point) and a new dart apex is marked onto the pattern piece. Then the new dart is extended up from the original seam line/base line notches, thus making a new dart. This can be seen clearly in Figs 116 and 117.

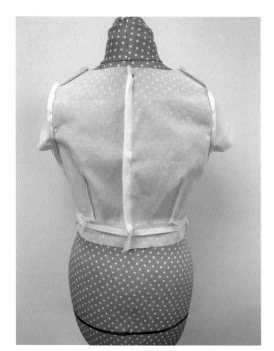

**Fig. 114 Toile turned inside out, showing the back seam taken in to remove excess fabric across the back of the bodice.**

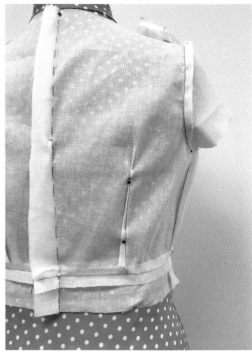

**Fig. 115 The darts are also lengthened slightly.**

**Fig. 116  Measuring by how much to increase the dart.**

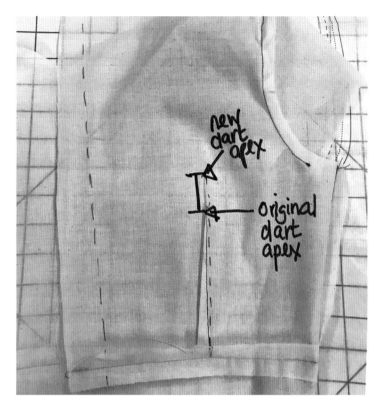

BELOW: **Fig. 117  New dart length drawn on pattern.**

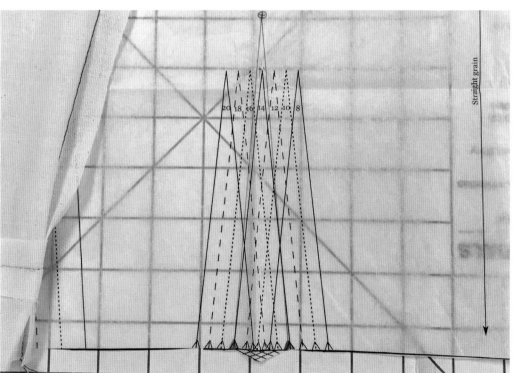

# Altering the Crotch Curve

Altering the fit of a pair of trousers is quite daunting for most of us, until we really understand what it is we are doing. We regularly read about increasing or decreasing 'the rise' and 'the crotch curve', but we're not always too sure why!

If the person being fitted has a curvy, round bottom, the crotch curve on the back of the trousers needs to be round and curvy too, so that it goes around the bottom nicely and meets the front of the trousers without straining. Someone with a flat bottom needs a much flatter curve in the back of the trousers.

Figs 118, 119 and 120 show the crotch curve being increased/made rounder. To do this, a new cutting line is being drawn inside the existing line and a French curve is used to draw the new cutting line onto the pattern tissue. You will see that different parts of the French curve are being used to redraw the new cutting line on the pattern tissue. Remember, you can use several parts of the French curve to get the best line, if you need to.

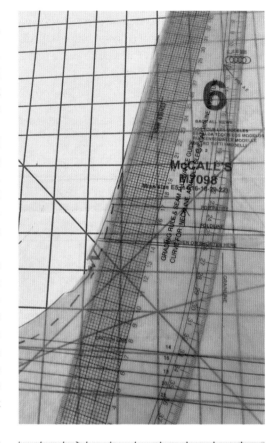

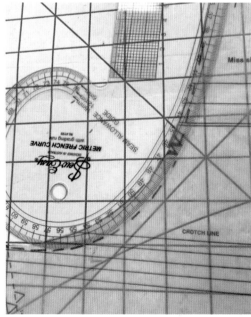

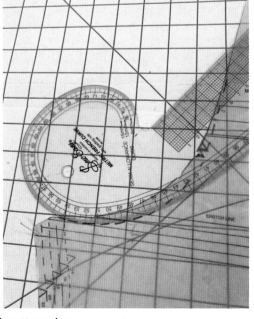

**Fig. 118  Using the French curve on the trouser back pattern piece.**

If you need to decrease the crotch curve/make it flatter, you will tape extra pattern tissue to the centre back seam and redraw the curve outside the existing pattern cutting line.

The front crotch curve of the trousers is equally important. If the crotch curve is too round and curvy, then the trousers may cut in too much and be uncomfortable when the wearer sits down. If the crotch curve is too flat and shallow, extra fabric will gather in vertical folds to either side of the front seam of the trousers. When this happens, the temptation is to pull at the side seams and try to reduce the extra fabric there, but that just pulls across the trousers and causes horizontal drag lines from the centre front seam out towards the hip.

So how do you know by how much to reduce or increase the crotch curve? There are several ways suggested for measuring crotch length, but this is a very personal measurement to take and not everyone is comfortable with either taking this measurement or with having it taken. One suggestion is to make small changes to the toile, either increasing or decreasing the curve, until the trousers are fitting much better. When you are increasing the curve or making it rounder, sew the new seam, unpick the old seam, snip the seam allowance and then try the trousers on again. If you are decreasing the curve or making it flatter, so long as you have enough seam allowance, make small decreases of 0.5cm or ¼in, unpick your original seam, press and refit the trousers. Once you have arrived at a good fit, then alter your paper pattern accordingly.

One important thing to remember when altering the crotch curve on trousers is that when you make the curve rounder/increase it, you are actually removing width from the trousers. So if you take in 1cm on the back curve, you should add 1cm in total to the side seam allowance on the trousers, if this appropriate to the fit of the trousers and according to the wearer's preference. If you reduce or flatten the curve, you will be adding width, so the side seam allowance may need to be taken in by the appropriate amount.

## Changing the Length

One of the most common calls for alteration is to the length. There are times when the length of a garment can be changed at the hemline, but only if a small adjustment is to

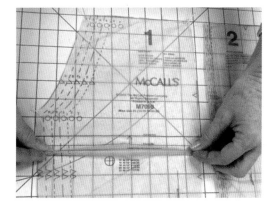

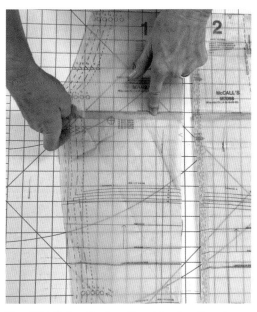

**Fig. 119   Using the lengthen/shorten lines to reduce the length of the front of the trousers.**

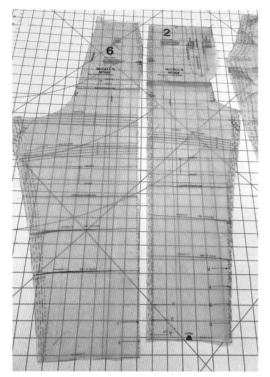

**Fig. 120   The length of the front and back pattern pieces is now different following alteration.**

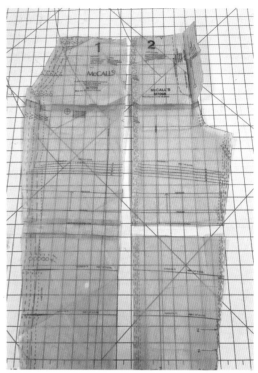

**Fig. 121   Adjusting the length further down the pattern piece.**

be made. Mostly it is best to use the lengthen/shorten lines on a pattern. The reason for this is that these lines are always placed where an adjustment will least affect the overall style of a garment. If you needed to lengthen an A-line skirt by several centimetres/inches and you did this at the hem of the skirt, you could end up with a skirt that is much more flared at the hem than you expected and that doesn't resemble the pattern design or your preferred style. However, if you alter the length at the lengthen/shorten lines, you will be able to make your adjustment without affecting the overall style of your skirt.

Fig. 119 shows the trousers demonstrated earlier in the book. The front of the trousers was a little too long for the model, from the waist to the crotch. It was therefore decided to shorten this area of the trousers. After this was done and

looking at all the pattern pieces, it could then be seen that the overall leg length had been changed, and now the centre front pattern pieces would not match the side front or the back leg of the trousers, as shown in Fig. 120.

Fig. 121 shows length being added back to the centre front leg, further down the pattern piece and just above the knee area, in order to return the centre front pattern piece to its original length and to make sure that the side seams will match when sewing the leg pieces together.

# Adjusting the Shoulders

Shoulder adjustments are very common, because many of us have one shoulder higher than the other, some of us are quite narrow across the shoulders, and some of us have very square or quite sloping shoulders. Whatever the reason for the shoulder adjustment, it must be tackled in stages, remembering again that no one solution will work for each fitting issue. Shoulder adjustments can also offer solutions for a gaping neck.

## Shoulder Adjustments and Gaping Neck

The dress worn by the model in Fig 122 was much too wide across the upper bust, neck and shoulders, causing gaping at the neck and around the armhole. The bust and shoulder seams were opened and the front shoulder area of the dress was moved to the left, thus eliminating the gaping neck. The result of this was that the princess seam over the bust had to be realigned and the front shoulder seam lengthened, as demonstrated in Fig. 123. The armhole cutting line has also been redrawn, because the adjustment to the front has moved the armhole to the left and it needs to be brought back to its original lines.

You may also see an instruction to 'add', written on the neck edge of the dress front. This instruction is indicating that width needs to be added at the neck edge of the front shoulder piece. You can just see the shoulder seam of the back of the dress under the model's hair. Because the centre front of the dress was moved to the left, the front shoulder seam is now much shorter than the back shoulder seam, so the neck edge of the shoulder, on the centre front panel, needs to be filled in and redrawn to fit the shoulder seam on the back of the dress.

All the alterations shown in Figs 122 and 123 were transferred to the paper pattern in the same way as described earlier in the chapter. Extra tissue was added to the paper pattern at the front neck edge and the front neckline was

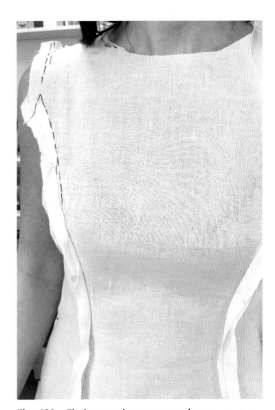

Fig. 122   Fitting a princess seam dress.

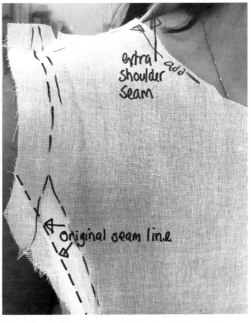

Fig. 123   Adjustments at the shoulder and at bust line.

redrawn so that the shoulder seams matched. Measurements were taken to show where the princess seam alterations started near the bust and where they finished on the armhole, and were copied onto the pattern. And the new armhole was also transferred onto the pattern.

This all sounds very complicated, but taking each step one at a time helps enormously!

## Shoulder Seam Adjustment

A lot of us have one shoulder higher than the other. So when we come to fitting our pattern, we might find that the shoulders don't lie very well and there is too much space between us and the dress on one shoulder! This might have the effect of making the top of the dress crumple slightly above the bust. A simple lift of the 'offending' shoulder seam can alleviate this problem and make the dress or bodice lie much

better. When doing this, be careful to check the armhole fitting after the shoulder seam has been lifted. If the alteration is significant, the armhole might become a little tight and may have to be opened out at the underarm. Remember also to alter only the shoulder seam that needs to be lifted.

Sloping shoulders may also need a shoulder seam adjustment. Again, pin out the alteration on the toile and check the fit of the armhole when the shoulder has been adjusted.

Sometimes a shoulder seam adjustment can get rid of a gaping neckline. Again, a simple lift at the shoulder seam may be all that is needed. Fig. 124 shows the dress bodice that we have seen earlier in the book being fitted on the dressform. When we examined the bodice front earlier, we could see that the V neck was gaping slightly. Fig. 124 shows that the left-hand shoulder seam has been opened and repinned. Only the front shoulder seam has been lifted, but this

**Fig. 124   Dress bodice with one shoulder lifted and the seam realigned.**

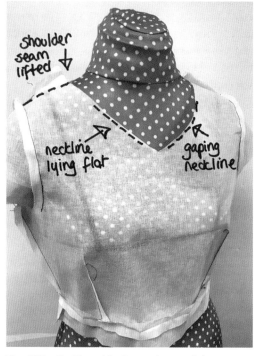

**Fig. 125   Getting rid of a gaping neck by altering the shoulder.**

has had the direct effect of removing the gape at the neck without causing any other fitting issues at all (*see* Fig. 125).

# Waist and Hip Width Alterations

How many of us go clothes shopping and struggle to find a skirt or pair of trousers that fit us around both the waist and the hips? Either the waist is too big but the skirt fits on the hips, or the waist fits well but the hips are too large! So it is with sewing at home and making our own clothes. We often find that we have to adjust the waist and the hip measurement on our patterns because we are not a standard size and they don't fit us too well in those areas.

If we are making a skirt or pair of trousers, we use our hip measurement as the key measurement for deciding which size of pattern to cut. Our hips are usually the widest part of our lower body. If, however, our tummy or abdomen measurement is bigger than our hip measurement, then the key measurement to use for selecting the pattern size will be the high hip (*see* Chapter 2: Cutting to Fit Tummy and Hips).

If the adjustment we need to make is not too large, we can use the multi-size cutting lines on the pattern and cut across different sizes in order to make a garment that fits us comfortably. This is demonstrated in Chapter 2: Cutting Across Different Sizes on Your Pattern Pieces. The principle is the same. You can move from one cutting line to another in order to get the fit that you need. Using the multi-size cutting lines, the waist can be cut one or more sizes larger than the hips, or the hips can be cut larger than the waist.

The same principle can be applied when making a dress or a jacket, or any other garment that hangs from the shoulders. If we find that the waist of our chosen pattern needs to be altered and we can use the multi-size cutting lines to do this successfully, then that is the easiest thing to do. If, however, we need to make a bigger adjustment to either waist or hips, we might have to add pattern tissue to the pattern piece to extend the waist or hip measurement slightly out beyond the maximum width of the pattern. In this case, pattern tissue can be added to the side of the pattern, but sometimes it's better to slice the pattern in two between the side seam and a front dart and extend the pattern there. You would then add to the width using the same method that you would use in adding to the length. Slide some pattern tissue in between the two pieces of your pattern. Fix one side of the pattern to the extra tissue and measure your increase all the way down. Then fix the other piece of pattern with tape. The result will be a skirt that fits your hips and tummy area better without changing the shape of the skirt and without moving the darts to the wrong place.

Some of these adjustments can be made to the pattern tissue before we cut the pattern pieces out and use them to make our toile. If we know our personal measurements well and we know that we always have to make a particular pattern adjustment, then making that adjustment before we cut the toile will ultimately save some time. If we are unsure about the alterations we will have to make, err on the side of caution; make sure you have measured well and have compared your measurements to the pattern pieces before cutting and sewing. This will also save time and disappointment. It's much better to cut slightly large and have to take our toile in, than for it to be too small and have to extend our pattern too much – or even worse, buy a new pattern and start again!

# FITTING ON A DRESSFORM

Many of us sew on our own at home, and although we may know other dressmakers, we might not know them well enough to be comfortable in asking them to fit a garment for us, or we are not sure about their ability to fit a garment in the way we would like. So how do we fit a garment on ourselves? We can use a dressform. A dressform can help hugely, once we have it sized properly to reflect our own measurements and shape. It also makes our sewing space look really good and works well as a clothes stand!

We need to choose the type of dressform carefully before we buy, and there is lots of choice out there. There are dressforms to fit the fuller figure or the smaller shape, to fit trousers and so on. Some may have narrower shoulders than others and many have different mechanisms for altering the size. Whatever dressform you choose, you will have to spend some time adjusting it to reflect your own size and shape as closely as you can.

Remember, however, that although using a dressform will really help you fit your garments, you must always try on your toile as well, just to make sure that your alterations are the best they can be for your fitting requirements.

## Sizing Your Dressform

Before you start using your dressform, you must make her (or him!) the right size for you.

Fig. 126 shows the dials used for changing the size of the dressform. There is a dial on the front of the dressform and there are measurement wheels on the side and back. There will also be a way of lengthening or shortening the dressform body at the waist. Locate this, because you will need it during the sizing process.

When the dial on the front of the dressform is turned to the required size for bust, waist and hip measurements, the dials on the side and back must also be turned. It is not enough to alter just the front or the back. But because there are dials on the front, the side and the back, this means that you can adjust for a wider or narrower back and a wider or narrower side measurement. For instance, if you are a 91cm/36in bust but you have a wide back, then you can open out the back of the dressform to say 96cm/38in, bring the side measurement down to 86cm/34in and leave the front dial at 91cm/36in. This should give you an overall 91cm/36in bust measurement on the dressform. You will need to use your personal body measurements to do this properly.

Likewise, if you have a narrow back, then reduce the back measurement, increase the side measurement slightly and either leave the front measurement dial at the correct bust size, or increase it if you have a fuller bust. The waist and hips can be adjusted in exactly the same way, filling out the tummy and pulling in the back of the dressform with the measurement dials to get the size that reflects your

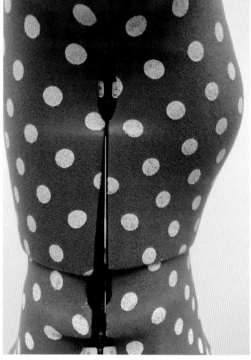

**Fig. 126   Size dials on a dressform.**

shape best. There is quite a lot of scope for changing the shape of the dressform, but always check with your tape measure that you have actually achieved the correct measurement on the dressform, as well as the correct shape.

After getting the size around your dressform almost to where you want it and before we start fine-tuning the size and shape of your dressform, you will need to make sure that she (or he!) has the correct back length. Remember, this is the length measured from the nape of your neck to your actual waist, not where you may prefer to wear your clothes. Lengthen or shorten the dressform according to your actual body measurements as per the personal body measurements diagrams described in Chapter 2.

# Fine-Tuning the Fit and Shape of Your Dressform

Now that you have adjusted all the dials on your dressform and have the back length where it should be, you might look at it and think that it still doesn't look anything like your shape at all. This is a bit disconcerting, so how do we fix it?

The first thing to do is to get an old bra that fits you very well and put it on your dressform.

You will notice immediately that even though your dressform is measuring your correct bust size, the bra is half empty! Take some wadding, or some kind of filler (old tights might work well), that will sit smoothly inside the bra and won't collapse when you put a garment on it or put some pins into it. Use the filler to pad out the bra slowly and carefully. Wadding can work well just inside the cup, and then use other fillers between it and the dressform. This helps to give the bra a little firmness so that you can pin onto it if need be. You will need to cut the wadding into shapes so that it lies more smoothly, and the wadding and filler will have to fill out the top of the cup more than the bottom of the cup. Once you have padded the bra, measure around the bust to make sure that your dressform is still matching your personal measurements. Use the dials to adjust the size up or down if necessary.

When you have done this, you must now measure from the shoulder down to the bust point/apex. Most dressforms don't allow us to move the bust up or down, so slide your 'padded' bra up or down slightly if you can, until you get the correct bust point/apex measurement for you. It may help to adjust the bra straps at the back to ensure that the bra is sitting better. Always measure as you go, and when you think you have everything as close as possible to your measurements, pin the top of the bra down into place so that it won't move. Now you should have a dressform that resembles your top half.

**Fig. 127  Getting the right bust shape on your dressform.**

Next, look at the tummy and hips on the dressform. Do they reflect your personal shape? If not, go back to your wadding and use pieces of it to pin to the hips, the tummy or the buttocks area until you get something that is beginning to resemble your shape more closely. Again, measure as you go, just to make sure you are not making your dressform too large. You will need careful waist and hip measurements for this and it will be necessary to ensure that if a fuller tummy is needed on the dressform, then the padding/wadding is fixed to the front of the dressform and not around the back as well. Again, use pins to hold the wadding in place. After this, a useful tip is to use Clingfilm! Wrap it over the wadding, and right around the dressform to completely cover the padding and secure it in place. You should still be able to pin a garment to the dressform through the Clingfilm, and it should hold everything nicely in place. Do the same for the hips, if needed.

Finally, how do we tidy our dressform up? Take a very close-fitting vest or lightweight top, or buy a dressform cover (as shown in Fig. 128). Put the top or cover on the dressform carefully, so that all your padding and alterations don't move out of place. Now you will have a dressform that is almost ready for you to use.

**Fig. 128  Sizing and shaping all done.**

## TIP: SEEING YOUR OWN BODY SHAPE

Ask someone to take a front view photograph and a side view photograph of you in a slip or close-fitting vest and leggings. Print the pictures and draw around your profile on them both with a marker pen. This will help you to see what your actual shape is and help you to pad out your dressform more accurately.

# Marking Key Measurements on Your Dressform

If you are going to the all the trouble of making your dressform resemble your personal shape, then there are a few more steps to take to have a really useful tool for fitting your future garments.

You will see in Fig. 129 that narrow tape has been applied to the dressform. These tapes are marking the key measurements of bust, waist, hips and bust point/apex.

Narrow tape has been pinned onto the dressform around the bust and then fixed in place with some small tacking/basting stitches to prevent it from moving. The same has been done for the waist. Note, this is the actual waist on the dressform and should be the same as our actual waist measurement. This is not where most of us choose to wear garments with a waist, as we tend to wear skirts and trousers below the waist for reasons of comfort. However, it is important when marking the dressform to mark the actual waist. The tape around the hip is also at exactly our hip placement position and is the correct distance from our actual waist (*see* the discussion on body measurements in Chapter 2). You may also want to mark your high hip if you have a fuller tummy and normally have to make fitting adjustments for it.

The final tapes over where the bra strap would lie are marking from the centre of our shoulder down to the bust point/apex. Again, this should be as accurate as possible on the dressform, if you are to successfully use her for fitting. It may be necessary to pull the bra up or down slightly to ensure that the measurement is correct and the bra is in the right place.

Another important measurement is from bust point to bust point. You must measure the distance between your bust points and fix your tapes to reflect that measurement. For some

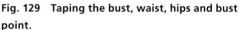

**Fig. 129  Taping the bust, waist, hips and bust point.**

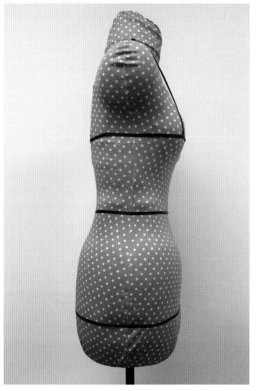

of us, our bust points are quite close together, while others have much more distance between right and left bust point. This impinges directly on how certain garments fit and where darts are placed. So make sure you get that measurement as accurate as possible.

Finally, you will see that when the dressform is turned sideways, all the tapes are parallel to the floor. This is very important, because they can now act as 'balance lines'. These are what some dressmaking fitters use to ensure that a garment is not pulling to the front, to the back or to one side. Balance lines help us to line up our garments on the dressform and on ourselves. They help ensure that our seams are hanging straight and that the bust, waist and hips are sitting correctly and in the right place.

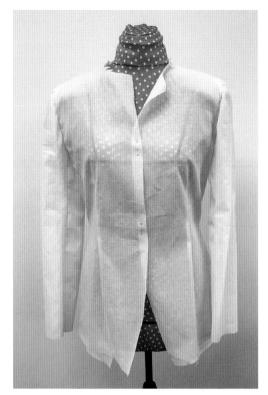

**Fig. 130   The marking tapes are visible through the jacket toile.**

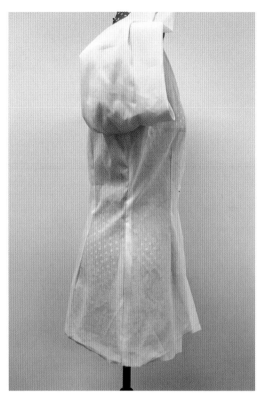

**Fig. 131   Using the tapes on the dressform to help with fitting the jacket.**

When you are putting a calico toile on the dressform, you should be able to see the tape lines showing through the calico and they will help you understand if darts are in the right place, if the shoulder is too wide or too narrow, if the waist needs to be dropped or raised and so on.

In Fig. 130 we can see the tapes through the calico. Looking at where the jacket sits in relation to the tapes, we know that the darts are placed quite well and are finishing just below and to the side of the bust point. We can see the waist tape and we can also see the hip tape, so we can understand better if the jacket is fitting well or if it needs to be altered. For example, the drag lines on the jacket, visible in Fig. 131, are centred around the waist and down towards the back hip area. We know this because we can see the waist tape underneath the jacket, and

the drag lines are pulling from above the waist tape to below it. This means that we will need to make an adjustment around the waist area of the side seam.

In Fig. 132, we can see the tapes quite clearly through the calico. Therefore, we can see that the darts from the waist up to the bust are actually too wide apart. Then, looking up to the neck and shoulders, it becomes clear that the dress bodice is possibly going to be too wide on the shoulder as well. Remember that a seam allowance around the neck will reduce the shoulder width at the neck edge by 1.5cm/⅝in and make the overall neck quite wide. In Fig. 133, one alteration has been made to the toile on the dressform and the results are that the darts have not needed to be altered at all, even though the issue with them was the first thing we noticed. The shoulder is now also in a

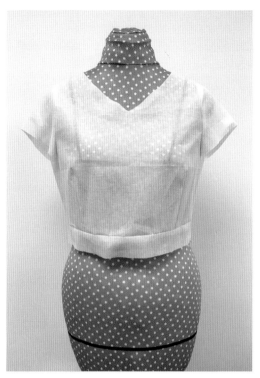

Fig. 132    The marking tapes are visible through the bodice toile.

Fig. 133    Using the tapes to make alterations to the bodice.

much better place. The alteration to the bodice comprised folding in a total of 2cm/¾in of the fabric down the centre front of the bodice. This is the part that was cut on the fold. The result is that the width of the bodice has been reduced very slightly overall, and this has had the double effect of moving the dart in slightly towards the centre of the body while also moving the neckline in slightly. The fit looks much better after this one small adjustment has been made on the dressform.

## TIP: USING THE DRESS-FORM FOR FITTING

Always, always, always try on your garment after fitting it on your dressform to make sure it does actually work for you!

The tapes on the dressform will help us to understand if our garment is proportioned properly and if we have to make any personal adjustments because of a high hip, a full tummy, uneven shoulders, garment length, dart position and so on. Mark and fix the tapes carefully, because once you get used to using the dressform and the tapes, they will help enormously with fitting garments on yourself.

If you decide to really 'get creative' and drape your own patterns onto the dressform, then those tapes are crucial guidelines for pattern creation on the dressform.

A word of warning – when your daughter asks you to make her a dress, think twice about changing your dressform for her. After all the time you have spent making the dressform right for you, changing it for her will be a big job. It will be much easier to invite her over on a regular basis for fittings.

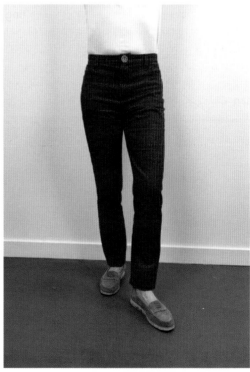

# GET CREATIVE!

Once the mystery has been taken out of fitting, then comes the opportunity for creativity. Understanding how to fit is a lot about understanding what pattern shapes are required to achieve different garment shapes. It's about understanding how two-dimensional pattern pieces are designed and then cut and stitched to make a three-dimensional garment. It's about learning what is required from a pattern piece to get a certain type of dart or fold or drape.

The more you fit and adjust your patterns, the more you will come to understand about pattern shapes, and ultimately some of the basics of pattern drafting. Pattern drafting involves designing garments on paper and then drafting all the individual pieces required to make the design. So to be able to draft a pattern, you need to understand what shapes can be sewn together to create a particular design outcome. The more you fit garments on people or your dressform, the more you will understand what those pattern shapes are.

Eventually you may come to the point where you want to make design changes to your patterns other than just fitting alterations. These design alterations may be small changes, or may be quite significant changes. You might make a short, straight cocktail dress into a long evening dress by lengthening the skirt and then adding a fishtail to the back seam. You might take a classic pair of trousers and change them into jeans or cut-offs or cigarette pants.

There are so many things you can do with your patterns to make them truly original and your own. You can change collars and cuffs, alter lengths, add waistbands. You can slash a T-shirt front and cut it into two pieces, add a seam allowance to the cut edge and make your T-shirt front in two different fabrics.

There is so much you can do. The only limiting factor will be your imagination. So go ahead, get confident with fitting and see where it takes you!

# GLOSSARY

| | |
|---|---|
| **Bust apex/bust point** | The most prominent point of the bust. |
| **Crotch depth/rise** | The distance from the waist to the bottom of the buttocks. |
| **Crotch length** | The total distance from back waist to crotch seam and up to front waist. |
| **Design ease** | The difference between body measurements and the finished garment measurements that the designer has specifically built in to the garment. |
| **Drag lines** | Folds created in a garment due to it pulling somewhere, usually because it is too tight. |
| **Dressform** | Tailor's dummy. |
| **French curve** | A tool used for drafting and altering patterns. It has graded curves, a straight edge and metric or imperial measures. |
| **Full bust adjustment (FBA)** | Increasing the bust/cup size on a pattern for a better fit, without altering the shoulder, waist and hip measurements. |
| **Lengthen/shorten lines** | Guidelines for where to increase or decrease the length of a pattern piece without affecting the overall shape of the garment. |
| **Line drawings** | The diagrams on a pattern envelope, usually on the back, describing the garment. |
| **Pitch points** | Points at which a pattern piece can be rotated, often to adjust the armhole or another curve. |
| **Small bust adjustment (SBA)** | Reducing the bust/cup size on a pattern for better fit, without altering the shoulder, waist and hip measurements. |
| **Stretch guide** | A measurement guide, usually found on the outside edge of the pattern envelope, to help decide if fabric has enough, too much or too little stretch for the pattern. |
| **Toile/muslin** | A fitting garment, made in calico or other suitable fabric, before sewing the final garment. |
| **True** | To realign seams and hemlines after alterations have been made to a pattern piece. |
| **Wearing ease** | The difference between body measurements and finished garment measurements that allow you to move in your garment and not be constrained by it. |

# INDEX